SELAH'S
Sweet Dream

Twelve-year-old Selah's quest to become an equestrian superstar is haunted by her grandmother's past and hindered by a horse with an attitude. She dreamed of a perfect sweet horse, but life is not a dream.

Dedication

*This book is dedicated to my granddaughter
who was born with a love of horses.*

I'm grateful to all who encouraged me along the way.

*To Janet, who read the roughest of first drafts and saw a gem. To
my amazing SCBWI critique group, The Critters: Charles, Mary,
Cheryl, Theresa, Carrie, Margaret, Vicki, and Alicia.*

*Thanks to my husband David, daughter Sarah, and son Christopher
for the constant encouragement.*

Glory to God. Every good and perfect gift comes from His hand.

Dear Reader:

Please, please share a review of this book.
Check my website for any ongoing contests or giveaways.
Sign up to be notified of the release of the next
horse adventure.

www.susancount.com
E-mail a comment: susancountauthor@yahoo.com

Follow Susan Count on Facebook:
www.facebook.com/susancount

Follow Susan Count on Pinterest:
www.pinterest.com/susancount

SELAH'S
Sweet Dream

SUSAN COUNT

CHAPTER ONE

*O*n the first day of another horseless summer vacation, Selah rehearsed the "horse talk" she planned to have with Grandpa. She gave it her best shot every summer. A horse would be no trouble. Grandpa had manicured pastures and a solid old barn.

For all of her twelve years, Selah had dreamed of a happily-ever-after life with a horse. She tucked her pale pink T-shirt into her jeans and stared at a poster-size canvas painting on her wall. In the painting, done by her grandmother, Selah was less than three feet tall and leading a brown and white paint horse in from the pasture. Even with only a rope around his neck, he followed her like an obedient dog.

Selah flipped her fingers through her cream-colored hair and bounced down the narrow, dark stairs of the farmhouse. The railing felt smooth with wear, and the boards groaned as if they'd prefer not to be disturbed. Finding no one in the house, she slipped out the screen door. Grandpa's dog, Skunk, didn't crawl out from under the porch so the dog was somewhere with Grandpa. As Selah tugged on her cowboy boots, she spotted the black-and-white Aussie dog, nose to the ground sniffing in the brush. Skunk was never far from Grandpa, so Selah strode up the hill toward her. The long and lush pasture grass darkened her pink boots with dew. Easing up beside Grandpa, she stayed quiet since he was quiet and peered into the thicket.

He motioned for her to step back from the edge of the woods with him. "Skunk brought me baby rabbits this morning. She could only carry one at a time, so she ended up dribbling a trail of bunnies down the hill. She must have thought they were puppies, and she should mother them. I followed her and her bunny trail all the way up the hill. She was happy to show me right where it was, so I returned them to the nest."

"What about their mother?" Selah tugged on his shirt.

"The doe will move them to a new nest when she finds they smell a little funny."

"How many are there?"

"I found four. Let's watch for more as we go back to the house." Grandpa put his arm across her shoulder and walked her away from the nesting area.

Skunk trotted before them weaving back and forth across the trail, down the hill. She stopped in midstride, picked up another baby bunny, and marched home with it.

"Skunk," Grandpa scolded.

With her head lowered, she marched on with a purpose.

"Skunk!" He slapped his camo cap on his knee. "Skunk is as determined to have her own way as you are, Selah."

Skunk paused and turned to look at him. He knelt down. "Come."

Her dark eyes watched him for a moment before she moved sluggishly to him.

Cupping his hands underneath her mouth, he told her to "give". In slow motion, Skunk released the bunny into his waiting hands.

"I understand, Skunk. Us girls need to stick together." Selah rubbed the dog's head. "Ahh... may I hold the baby, Grandpa?"

"Sure." He slipped it into her hands. "Got it?"

"Oooow, its eyes aren't even open yet." She stroked its fur with one finger. "Soft as silk. Everything about the bunny is adorable. Look at its teeny, tiny nose. I thought its tail would be fluffy, but it's bald." Selah tilted her head to the side and flashed Grandpa her most irresistible smile. "May I keep it?" She cuddled the bunny near her cheek.

"That wouldn't be the best thing for the baby, now would it?"

"No, I guess not, but I love bunnies." The smile faded from her face. "Its mother can take better care of it than I could."

"Good thinkin'."

"But I would take such good care of a horse," Selah blurted.

He rotated to look at her as his face scrunched up. "Not again, Selah. Don't push me on that."

"Grandpa! You've seen the walls in my room at home. Every inch is covered in horse. Why can't we just talk about getting a horse?"

"Because I said so."

"The farm's too quiet, Grandpa. A horse farm should be alive with horses."

"I'm done with horses, Selah."

"I need a horse of my own! You know Grandma would've wanted me to have a horse."

His eyes darkened. He wagged a finger at her, and then shoved his hands in his pockets as he turned back toward the nest. "Selah, that's enough. Bring the bunny and come on. Your summer vacation should not be torture for me. Do you want me to call your parents and have them come get you already?"

"No, sir. But, it's your fault! You gave me Grandma's horse library. Do I read anything except horse books?"

"She would have wanted you to have them."

"And a horse!" Selah bit the inside of her lip. "When I was really little and your paint horse put his muzzle right in my face, and breathed his scent on me... it's like he cast a spell over me that changed me forever."

"I'm sorry, Selah. It's not gonna happen. I let you get a cat, remember? And I ended up taking care of it. I don't even like cats."

"You love Pearl." She eased the last baby in with its litter as she glared at Grandpa.

Some clouds moved in over the Canaan Grasslands of Texas. They looked a lot like flying, dark horses. She should get back to the house before Grandpa started to worry. A bee buzzed her shoulder. She whisked the little bother away, snapped another of her grandmother's horse books shut, and tossed it into her pink backpack. Concentrating on reading was tough when she could hear Grandpa like he was standing right next to her saying "Do you want me to call your parents and have them come get you already?"

She clenched her fists and faced toward the farm. "I'm not giving up. We need to work on our plan for getting a horse, Skunk."

Picking her way along the grassy path, she climbed to the top of the knoll. She fingered the top of Skunk's head and stopped to look at the sun moving lower in the sky. Selah looked out over the expanse of the Grasslands behind Grandpa's farm. She'd done a lot of growing up here and whiled away many hours exploring its woods and surrounding meadows.

"What's that?"

Straining to see, she couldn't quite make out anything except a dark shape. Selah slipped to a nearby tree, dropped her backpack, and used it like a stool to swing up on the lowest branch just like the monkey bars. She stood on the branch. "There's something out there," she whispered down to the dog. From her perch, she still couldn't quite distinguish the dark shape until its head popped up from the grass.

"A horse?" Questions sprang into her mind in rapid fire. Where did it come from? How did it get here? As her foot slipped, she lunged for the branch overhead, gripping the rough bark. Some skin scraped away from her hands. Her body swung, and she smacked into the tree trunk, nearly losing her grip. Her feet scrambled for the branch below.

As her attention returned to the horse, its body snapped alert as if it heard something scary. In the next instant, it exploded into a run as if its life depended on speed. The galloping horse disappeared behind a stand of trees. Selah stretched as high as she could on the branch to catch one more glimpse.

"It can't be. Or are you the sweetest dream I've ever had?" she questioned. "But you saw it, didn't you, Skunk?"

Skunk sprawled in the grass with her head nestled on her paws. Her soft, glistening eyes watching her playmate in a tree.

Selah slithered down the tree and slung her pack onto her shoulder as she ran to the farm. Every stride pumped the phrase, "I saw my horse!"

As she burst through the farmhouse door, the door slammed against the wall and bounced back at her. Selah searched the kitchen and utility room. "Grandpa! Grandpa!"

His feet thudded on the wooden floors as he hurried to find her. "Selah?" he called back in alarm. "Are you all right?"

Completely out of breath, she sputtered, "Yes." She sucked in air and panted. "I found a horse."

He sank into the nearest chair. "For goodness sake, Selah, you scared me to death. Was that really necessary?"

"I'm sorry, Grandpa, but I found a horse in the Grasslands."

"Well, that's strange." His fingers squeezed the skin on his chin. "It can't be a wild horse. There haven't been wild horses around here in my lifetime. If you saw a horse, it must belong to someone."

"I did. I did see a horse. But it was too far away to tell much about it except that it can run like the wind and it's black."

"You have an overactive imagination." With a quick flip of his head toward the stairs, he sighed. "Go wash up. It's time for dinner. Why is there blood on your hands?"

"Oh, it's nothing. I scraped my hands on some bark. I'm too excited to eat. Just think of it—a beautiful, beautiful horse out there somewhere." Pressing her face against his soft denim shirt, she gave him a quick hug, and then dashed up the stairs to her room where she twirled around and flopped on the bed. Dreams of horses swirled in her mind.

"God? Did you hear my prayer?" She clamped her hands over her eyes to shut out the other possibility. "Or is Grandpa right and it's my imagination?"

CHAPTER TWO

*T*he next morning thunder shook the old house while the rain pelted the roof. Dismayed, Selah stared out the window. She couldn't go look for the horse in this weather. Grandpa would be steamed. He'd gone to run errands and said he'd be back late. Selah wanted to stay at the farm so if the rain broke she could go to look for the horse.

For hours, rain battered the house. Even when it let up for a moment, it still looked gray and angry outside. She paced in her room. She couldn't concentrate to read. How could a day be so long?

She needed to find something to do before she drove herself crazy. A movie? The old house's creaky stairs made the stairwell feel haunted as she eased down them. The thunder passed, but the rain dumped down in buckets.

She clicked on the TV and scrolled through the movies. Nothing looked interesting. Finally finding an old movie about a racehorse and a girl in a wheelchair, she selected and paused it. She headed to the kitchen to make popcorn. Skunk's eyes followed her as she passed by.

"Rest up, Skunk. I'm counting on you to help me find my horse."

As Selah moved through the hallway with her popcorn, her eyes shifted to some home movie tapes pushed to the back of a bookcase. She squinted to read the faded writing on the label, but couldn't make a logical word out of it.

Selah took one of the tapes into Grandpa's dusty and slightly musty office. She shoved aside a stack of books and papers to uncover the input portal on the ancient player. It sprang to life with a quiet whirl, and Selah's grandmother filled the screen.

"I miss you, Grandma." Selah's eyes flickered to her grandmother's picture on the desk and back to the screen. Grandma was riding her dressage mare. Beautiful, long-legged, black elegance as they moved together in perfect rhythm and… harmony.

"Harmony. That was the mare's name." How perfect they were together. "I wonder what happened to the mare." Turning up the music, Selah watched the pair dance a musical freestyle—pure grace in motion. The tape fluttered, and the image blackened.

She was about to push the eject button when the video flickered back on again. Selah caught her breath. She'd know the horse in the round pen anywhere. His portrait hung on the wall of her room at the farm. In the video, nothing tied the paint horse and Grandpa together. Grandpa directed the horse's movements with subtle signals. They looked like ballroom dancers. "Grandpa loved that horse more than I did. Why did he send him away?"

"Smells like a movie theater in here. Hope you made popcorn for me, too," bellowed Grandpa as he let the backdoor bang.

"In here, Grandpa."

He walked into his office and started to reach out for a handful of popcorn. "What are you doing in my office?" His arm froze in the air when he saw the video playing of his beloved show horse.

Watching pain pool in his eyes, Selah hit the off button.

As though struck dumb, he stared at the now-blank screen. He pulled his cap off his full head of freshly trimmed silver hair, sighed heavily, and dropped in the desk chair like a ton of bricks. A long moment passed, and then, as if a light came back on, he said, "I asked Al, my barber, if he knew anything about a loose horse in the Grasslands. He knows everything that happens around town."

Selah leaned toward Grandpa and listened, willing him to talk faster as her eyes bored into him.

"Al didn't see how the horse you saw could be the same one he heard about a couple years back. He said there was a black, two-year-old filly in a horse trailer that had jackknifed on Highway 75 about twenty miles south of Athens. The filly pulled away from the deputy holding her by the side of the road and bolted down the highway. They searched the Grasslands for weeks, but came up empty."

"So someone would want her back?" Selah clasped her sweaty hands together, and her fingertips squashed into her knuckles.

"Yes, sunshine. They would, if it's the same horse."

"Can we go out and look for the horse tomorrow?"

"No, we should call the sheriff's office tomorrow and turn it over to them. They'll have the resources to deploy in a search. We shouldn't get involved."

"Oh please, Grandpa, can we go look for it? I just know *you* could find it. Wouldn't we be doing a good thing for the horse?" He pressed his fingers into the tabletop and drummed his pointer finger. She hadn't convinced him yet. Selah slipped her hand under Grandpa's. "If you lost something you loved, wouldn't you want someone to help you look for it?"

No immediate response drew another plaintive plea. "Please…"

He nodded in slow motion. "You are incorrigible. Sometimes, I think you could get me to go over Niagara Falls in a barrel." He hugged her and kissed the top of her head. "Don't you go getting any ideas, though. You can't keep it."

Offering him her popcorn bowl, she asked with care, "What happened to Grandma's horse?"

Grandpa looked out the window and didn't answer.

Selah waited.

His chest heaved with a sigh, and he refocused on her. "I gave her to a dear friend of your grandma's, who loved the mare and wanted to raise colts out of her. Harmony's in a brood mare herd and won't be going back into competitions again. It was what your grandma would have wanted for both of her dearest old friends."

Selah hung on his every word without interrupting.

"Laura takes great care of Harmony, and Harmony lives the good life. She's given Laura several fine foals. One of the youngsters made the Olympic Dressage Team a few years back. Laura named the horse MaryMary after your grandma."

"I remember her. She was phenomenal, Grandpa." With a quiet breath, she asked, "Where did the paint horse go?"

Grandpa stared at the hat in his hands. "It's been a long day, Selah. I'm going to turn in."

CHAPTER THREE

*D*evouring her cereal so breakfast wouldn't delay the search, Selah looked up from the laptop on the kitchen table. "I don't find any water in the Grasslands with Google Earth."

"Keep looking. In order for this horse to have survived all this time, there's got to be a pond or something." He stuffed his backpack with things Selah gathered for their search. A GPS, a halter, lunch, water, and duct tape, of course. Grandpa never, ever left home without duct tape. "Selah, do you have carrots in your pack?"

"Yes." She considered saying something about maybe the lost horse would need a home, but decided... naah... bad timing. "Look at this, Grandpa. Could this be a little pond under the tree cover?"

Peering at the screen and studying the images, he pursed his lips and wrinkled his forehead. "Could be, but it's not real clear, is it?

Is that the best option?"

"It looks like the only option. I just don't see anything that looks like water."

"Let's head out in that direction. If we can find a pond, then we can check the area for hoofprints. The tricky part of getting there will be going through this wooded section. See the dry gullies?" He traced his finger along a shadow on the screen. "I'm betting they are deep and steep." Skunk snoozed on the doormat. "Those gullies might be more than we can navigate without a little help from our sleeping friend. I'll toss in some rope, too."

When they stepped out onto the porch, the morning was still and quiet. The sky had a kiss of lavender. Skunk rose up off her mat, stretched, and yawned. Grandpa took up his twisted walking stick and led the little search party off on their mission to find a horse. If there even was a horse.

Selah stayed unusually quiet and focused. Her eyes scanned every conceivable spot where a horse could hide. Every moving thing came under her intense scrutiny. Nothing turned out to be a lost horse, however.

Skunk started barking like a maniac.

Selah searched the thicket for any sign. "Did you find my horse, Skunk?" she whispered.

Lunging at the edge of the woods, Skunk flushed out a fawn. Seeing the cause of her great alarm, she whined but stood at alert, as if to chase the baby.

"It's okay, Skunk. We're all tired." Grandpa collared her. "Time for a break. Want some lunch, Selah?"

While a sandwich sounded yummy, having to stop was annoying. Her eyes never stopped scanning the meadow while she ate. "Where…are you?"

After lunch, they hiked on, toward the spot they'd identified as most likely to be water.

Grandpa studied the GPS screen. "We aren't far now." Without looking up, he pointed to the north. He zeroed in on his target. "My best guess is we need to go through the heavy brush by that sycamore tree. The gully should be about three hundred feet beyond the tree."

Selah tromped through the woods, pushing aside the low-hanging branches. With her thumb and first finger, she lifted away some thorny, thick vines. "Ouch." A vine tangled in her hair, biting into her head. Reaching higher, she gripped the vine and pulled her hair free, strand by strand. "Ouch," she said again, louder, sucking blood off her finger. A ribbon of blood dripped down her forehead and over the bridge of her nose. Sliding a damp wipe out of her pack, she held pressure on the wound and hurried to catch up with Grandpa.

"This way, Selah. This looks like a deer trail." Soon, they came to the rim of the "dry gully". Grandpa was right: it was formidable.

"Didn't you say the gullies were dry?" Selah questioned, pondering the muddy slop in the bottom of the ravine.

"Silly rabbit. A 'dry gully' is a ditch that channels water away after a rain."

"Oh, so it's dry—unless it rains. That's stupid—just sayin'."

He nodded as he tied off a rope on a tree at the gully's edge. Gripping the line, he eased himself down the steep bank.

Selah picked her way behind him. She balanced warily on an oak log wedged across the bottom of the ravine to cross over the yucky brown water.

Skunk slopped and splashed through the water to Grandpa. He told her to "take it" as he put the rope in Skunk's mouth. "Hold."

He directed her to go up the steep bank. She slipped, slid, and struggled, but made it. Grandpa encouraged her to go around a tree nearby and bring the end of the rope back down to him.

"What a smart girl," he sweet-talked to her. "Here, Selah, take this rope and tie it off on the root of the tree by you." He tugged on the secured rope, and then used it to pull himself up the other side of the gully.

Selah grabbed the rope and pulled herself about halfway up the steep ravine when both of her feet slipped out from under her. She fell flat on her belly in the mud and gunk, but she gripped the rope like a lifeline so she didn't slide into the water. There must be snakes hiding in that mucky muck.

Selah looked up at him as she struggled to her knees and coaxed her feet to where they belonged. When his lips twitched, she knew he was trying not to laugh at her "pink" covered in mud. A faint streak of blood slipped down her forehead and nose. With her jaw tensed and her feet planted on solid ground, she said, "Mud and blood won't keep me from looking for my horse." Wiping the grime from her hands across the butt of her jeans, she called, "This is pretty rough. Could a horse get through here?"

"Don't think so. It's had awhile to pick a better trail if there is one."

"You believe me, don't you, Grandpa? You believe I saw a horse?"

"Yes, sunshine, I guess I do. Call it a hunch, but I think you saw the black filly that disappeared a couple years ago."

Selah smiled. *When we find the horse, I will find a way to make her mine.*

The rain from the night before turned the ground soft around the little, dark pond in the woods. If the horse came here for water, it would be easy to spot its prints.

Selah's voice bubbled with excitement when she spotted the many footprints. "Look for a hoofprint."

"Selah, come see. This split hoof here, that's a deer. The print next to it looks like a large coyote with a couple pups. There's a raccoon print."

Her finger traced the coyote track. "Yeah, but, do you see any hoofprints?"

Grandpa looked long and hard before he shook his head. "No, not one. We suspected those gullies must surround this water hole. They'd make it hard for a horse, though the deer seem to get in here okay. Let's head back, and we will look again at Google Earth."

Discouraged and tired, Selah plodded after her grandpa. "I was so sure we would find some trace here."

They trekked home without much to say, all the while keeping a watchful eye out for any sign of the horse.

It was pitch-dark by the time they dragged themselves onto the porch. Pearl meowed, rubbed on Selah's leg, and went to wait by the door for her dinner. Pearl had to eat first, or there'd be no peace in the house. Selah slumped into the first chair and tugged off her boots. She brushed more dry mud from her favorite horse T-shirt, relieved she didn't get blood on it. Grandpa went straight to the cabinet to get dinner for Skunk. And if dog food smelled good, then it was definitely time to make some dinner.

Selah whipped up some scrambled eggs—the only thing she knew how to cook.

Grandpa flipped open the laptop and searched the area again for a watering spot. "Zip, zilch, zero." He frowned, looking more than a little confounded. "I'm stumped."

"Can we go out again tomorrow and keep looking?"

He shook his head. "No. I have a doctor's appointment tomorrow morning. That horse has been hiding out there for a long time now, and it just might stay that way."

Too tired to figure out how to persuade him otherwise, Selah kissed his rough cheek. "Thanks, Grandpa, for going out with me today." She trudged up the stairs without the joy she had expected to have by now. It'd been a long, long day with nothing to show for it.

"The Lord knows where my horse is hiding," she whispered as she eased the loft bedroom door closed.

CHAPTER FOUR

After my appointment, I'll stop by the sheriff's office to tell him about the horse. I'll be home right after lunch." Grandpa poured out a cup of coffee. "We could drive up to Athens later and catch a movie."

Selah heard, but didn't register. All she could think about was where the horse might be. A movie? Naa, nothing was more important than finding the horse.

She tried to wait for him to come home so she could talk him into going back out to search. "Waiting is driving me crazy. I've got to go. I know you are out there somewhere, and I've got to find you." She heard a whisper deep inside her... *before it's too late.*

She pulled the halter from Grandpa's pack and stuffed it into her own, next to the bag of carrots and her small pair of binoculars.

Dashing off a quick note to Grandpa, she called to the dog. "Let's go, Skunk."

With new spring to her step, and a whispered prayer on her lips, she carried hope like a banner as she marched out of the farmyard.

About thirty minutes into the hike, she remembered she was supposed to call Mom this morning. She paused on the trail. She hadn't talked to her mom and dad since she got to Grandpa's on Sunday. "I can't go back. I've got to do this. Will Mom understand?"

Skunk stopped on the trail, tilted her head, and peered back at her. "Are ya comin?" she seemed to say. When Selah didn't move, Skunk came to her and laid down in the middle of the trail. Skunk moved her paw to rest on Selah's foot and made the most endearing little "aarall" sound.

"You feel it too, don't you, Skunk? Something is wrong, and we need to find our horse."

The well-worn, familiar trail comforted her. Along these paths, Grandpa had shown her the glory of God. He'd taught her to marvel at nature's intricate detail. The time they came across a red and black velvet cow ant, he spent twenty minutes squatted by the trail with her.

Selah looked out over the meadow's color of the week. One week the flowers, as far as she could see, were purple and yellow. A few weeks later, white blanketed the same field.

Grandpa had told her, "The meadows are a picture of the Lord, reminding us each day is like a flower. And our life is a bouquet."

Buzzards circled in the distance.

"They're after some poor thing that's died." Following a sharp intake of her breath, she blurted, "I hope it's not the horse. We should go look-see."

Holding onto Skunk's collar, Selah moved toward where the buzzards gathered.

Goose bumps crept up Selah's neck and arms. "It's black. It's my horse, Skunk!" Fear and panic gripped her heart. "It's down. But it's moving. It's alive."

The horse was still a football field length away. The buzzards got braver by the moment.

"If they get to the horse before we do, they could take its eyes out. This is horrible."

Selah tripped on Skunk's foot, and the dog yelped but labored against the collar to get to the buzzards.

"Nasty birds. Get away from my horse!" Trying to hurry, but not make things worse, Selah approached as fast as she could. "I don't know what to do, Skunk. If I send you to chase the buzzards, it might panic the poor horse."

The horse's ears pivoted toward Selah and Skunk. It thrashed and struggled to get up. Even with a great heave of effort, it only managed to exert itself before toppling back on its side.

As they edged closer, the buzzards scattered. Intimidated by her and Skunk's presence, they hopped a few feet away. She flapped her one free arm at them.

Barking, Skunk strained against her collar. Then, as if on one wing, they lifted off the earth like an evil, black cloud.

Selah turned to the downed horse. It was snorting, and its eyes flared wide with fright. A mass of wire coiled around its front legs. One hind leg was stretched forward and bound to the front legs.

"Thank you, God, that we got here in time." Selah inched closer, talking in a quiet voice to the stricken animal. She was instantly smitten and star-struck. "Oh, you are so beautiful. Are you for real or am I dreaming? Easy there. We are here to help you, if we can. Pretty, pretty thing," Selah cooed soothingly as she looked into the horse's panicked eyes. Fear stared back at her.

"You are everything I ever dreamed you would be. What happened to you?" The horse's legs had streaks and mats of blood. Her mane and tail were knotted and twisted. No matter, she looked perfect, in spite of her obvious lack of care. "Easy, girl. Let us help you."

The buzzards gathered around in little clusters, some on the ground and some perched in the nearby trees like scary Halloween decorations. Their heads were gray-black with a texture that looked like an orange peel. Something smelled putrid.

The mare was on high alert and tense. Her ears flickered independently checking out the danger on all sides. The buzzards began to crowd in again. The horse blasted a sharp, loud snort, which startled Selah and blew the buzzards back. A short standoff ensued until one of the enormous birds spread and lifted its wings. It took a couple of awkward hops toward the mare. From its long, revolting, hooked beak came a raspy hiss.

As it postured aggressively, Selah screamed, "Skunk! Get 'em!" Selah flapped her arms and continued to yell. The horse thrashed to free itself, and the whites of its eyes showed pure panic.

Skunk charged the black nightmare of a bird, growling like she was vicious. Apparently her act was convincing because the horrible bird retreated back with the others. Skunk stood with her fur raised up all along her back and neck and did a little posturing of her own.

"I'm sorry I scared you, pretty thing, but I had to do something. We've got to get you out of this tangle fast." She'd need more than the carrots she'd packed. "I need some wire cutters."

Selah dropped cross-legged to the ground. "What should we do, Skunk? I can't unwrap the wire; she is too scared for that." She looked around as if help might magically materialize.

"We can't leave you because the buzzards will come back for you. I've only told my parents a hundred times I need a phone." As Selah considered what to do, Skunk sank down on her belly and inched her way up to the terrified horse. The horse stretched up her neck as high as she could and cocked her head to look down at the furry predator, which was not acting much like a predator.

At that moment, the solution seemed obvious. "Skunk, you stay with the horse. I will run home as fast as I can."

"No worries, beautiful girl, Skunk will watch over you till we can get you out of this mess." Selah explained to the horse, hoping to elicit cooperation from the mare. "Stay, Skunk. And I'll be back," she said over her shoulder as she struck out for the farm. She alternated running with walking to cover as much ground as possible. She tried not to think about what might happen if she took too long. The buzzards were waiting for their opportunity.

"Skunk is in charge, and she is the smartest farm dog there ever was. Please, God, watch over my horse and Skunk."

Grandpa's blue truck was parked in the driveway as Selah sprinted into the farmyard. She started yelling for him the instant she saw the truck. His head popped out from around the door to his shed.

"Wire cutters. I found her, Grandpa! She is real." Selah slowed to a jog. "She's all tangled. The buzzards are after her. We scared them away." She bent over and put her hands on her knees, but kept pouring out the news. "Skunk's guarding her. We have to hurry, Grandpa."

"Wait. Slow down a bit. Get a breath. I can't understand you." He handed her a bottle of water. "You saying you found a horse?"

Turning to rummage through a messy drawer, he didn't seem to hear Selah's faint reply, "I found my dream horse."

He found a pair of mean-looking wire cutters and handed them to her. "Let me grab my pack, and we can head back out."

In less time than it took to fry an egg, they moved out with Selah in the lead. Both were quiet and focused. They used all their energy for covering ground.

As they approached, the horse raised her head in attention. She gave one quick, alarmed snort. Skunk, doing an admirable job, rested in the shade about ten feet from her charge. The buzzards had given up and gotten lost.

Grandpa crossed his arms across his chest and sputtered out a deep breath. He scratched his head, reached for Selah's hand, and drew her along with him. They advanced slowly and smoothly. "She got herself in quite a pickle. Lucky for her you went on out this morning. This horse is totally helpless." He stopped and patted her hand. "There sure is a lot of blood everywhere, but I don't see any gushing."

"Why is there a pile of wire out here anyway?" Selah asked.

"Could be part of an old fence, and this got left behind when they cleaned up. Or it might have fallen off the ranger's four-wheeler. But leave it to a horse. If there is a way for them to hurt themselves, they'll find it."

"Well, let's get her out of this mess."

"Alrighty then, I'm going to put a halter on and cut off the wire. You have to hold her down." He knelt down by their packs and pulled things out.

Selah stood transfixed by the wonder of the mare. "You're for real—for real."

He eased up to the mare and slipped the halter on her head in one easy, practiced manner. "I'm going to lay her head down now, Selah. I need you to ease around behind her. You will lie across her neck to keep her head down. But be alert. If she starts to struggle, it could be dangerous for you. If that happens and you don't think you can hold her, I want you to get away from her—fast."

"Will she bite me?"

"She will try to defend herself any way she can, so watch yourself. I'll hold her down until you are in place."

Selah eased closer to the mare to get in position, ready to do her part.

"Just put the love from your heart in your hand, and move it over her neck and shoulders," he encouraged her. "That's the smartest horse trick I ever learned. It'll help her to trust you."

Selah concentrated on his instructions.

"Keep your weight on her neck and don't touch anything on her head while I work on her legs. Stick to her neck and shoulder, withers and back."

Selah's eyes darted to Grandpa, and she nodded that she understood.

The mare's coat didn't feel soft like Selah had imagined. Small lumps lurked under her skin on her chest and neck. Her mane was long, but a straggly mess. Masses of scars blemished her body.

"You're still the most beautiful, perfect creature I have ever seen," Selah whispered.

With Grandpa crowding close and Selah draped over her neck, the mare's ability to process what was happening to her was undone by her stress. The horse struggled, and Selah fought to stay in position. Holding her own, Selah kept the horse's head down. She did as Grandpa instructed. She put her heart in her hand and rubbed the mare with love. Smiling with delight, she cooed words only the two of them understood. The mare rewarded Selah's efforts by being still. Selah could feel the mare's tight muscles underneath her, but the horse lay as if frozen.

Selah soothed and quieted the mare with her gentle voice. Grandpa whipped out his duct tape and secured her front feet together so she wouldn't free herself prematurely when she struggled. Then he set to work on the twisted wire. He gently worked as much of it as possible away from the wounds on her legs. The mare's body responded with a jolt of involuntary reflex every time the wire cutters snapped.

The legs were tender and bruised and had several gashes. With the wire free, but her feet still taped together, he applied antibiotic to the worst gashes. Selah fingers caressed the mare's neck. Grandpa pressed a piece of gauze on a deep wound and secured it with elastic wrap.

He looked up from his handiwork and smiled at Selah. "We have to do this together now. I will count to three. I want you to slide off her neck and get back away from her. I am going to cut the tape off her hooves. Since she hasn't been handled in a long time, I'm expecting a bit of a rodeo after all this trauma. I want you out of the way."

"Got it." Selah nodded, thinking hard.

"One. Two. Three." He cut her loose. She lay still for a minute, and then tested to see if all the wire was gone. She pushed up on her front legs and sat awkwardly. Pulling her hind legs underneath, she struggled like a newborn foal to get up from the ground.

The little group stood stock still. Grandpa, poised as though expecting an explosion just any minute now, had a firm grip on the lead rope. The standoff continued. Selah held her breath, waiting and hoping.

Ever so slowly, the little mare stretched her neck out and forward toward Selah.

"You have a carrot to give her?" Grandpa asked. "She's got to be hungry. She's been down long enough to eat everything green around here that she could reach."

Moving carefully, never taking her eyes off the mare, Selah extracted a carrot and held it out.

The horse snatched and crunched the offered carrot.

Selah grinned. "I think she remembers that people feed her even though she has run free for so long."

The greedy horse devoured carrot after carrot until Grandpa pointed out, "It would be good to save a few in case we need persuaders on the walk home."

With that, he coaxed the horse to take a step forward. The mare leaned back against the halter while she lightened her forequarters and hobbled forward a step. It was a painful step for Selah to watch.

"I'm encouraged. She seems to remember she's halter broken. She responds when I ask her to take a step," Grandpa said.

Selah grimaced. "Ah, it hurts her so."

"I hope walking will help her loosen up. If that is the best she can do, we will be stuck out here. Dig in the bottom of my pack,

Selah, and look for a white tube marked Bute. It's pain medication. Even if she does take it, the effects won't be immediate. But it might mean we can get her home instead of having to sleep out here, in the grass, with her tonight."

Selah plucked a tube marked apple-flavored Bute from the pack and handed it to Grandpa. He stepped to the horse's side and slipped it in the corner of her mouth before she knew what was happening. She objected for only a moment, and then smacked her lips deciding it tasted good.

"She's hungry if she likes Bute. The way to her heart is definitely through her stomach," he said.

They continued, one painful step at a time, and soon enough, the walking itself loosened up the sore muscles and tendons. When the Bute kicked in, they'd make faster progress.

Grandpa pulled his phone out of his pocket. "Is Dr. Steve there? I'll wait…. Doc, can you make my place your last stop at the end of the day? Good, thanks. Selah found the mare that has been in the Grasslands for a couple years, and we are heading into the farm…. Yeah, hard to believe, isn't it? She got tangled in some fence wire and is pretty cut up. We are making our way in with her now, but at this rate, it could be pretty late in the day…. I'll do that, thanks. Bye."

He turned to Selah. "Dr. Steve will meet us at the farm about five o'clock, or we are to call him if we can't get in by then. If she doesn't walk better with the Bute, you and Skunk will go to the farm and bring him back to meet us. He can give her something stronger for pain so we can bring her on in."

The rescue party and the rescued treasure pressed on together. "She is perfect. Thank you, God." Selah squealed with glee. In that split second, the mare snaked her head toward Selah. Grandpa jerked the lead line sharply, and Selah leapt out of the way. "She didn't mean it," Selah assured him.

"She absolutely meant every word of it. Be more careful and stay farther away." He scowled at the horse.

They were close enough now to the farm to see the setting sun glinting off the barn's silver roof. The mare hobbled a little faster now, but it was still slow going. Blood from her wounds soaked her bandage and oozed down her front legs.

Selah kept feeding little bits of carrots to keep the horse in a cooperative frame of mind. She never missed an opportunity to stroke the mare, but the horse flinched at her touch. Playing it safe, Selah stayed away from the hooves and teeth that Grandpa warned could flash out in an instant.

As he watched her extend a carrot, his eyes softened. "Selah, don't give up your heart to this mare. We still have to call the sheriff and have him track down the owners. We can't keep her."

"I can't help it, Grandpa. Deep in my heart, I know she's meant for me."

"Whoa there. You're getting way ahead of yourself. We can't keep her. She belongs to someone." He paused and then added, "Not that I don't understand. Something about her captures your heart. It's almost as if... I should know her."

CHAPTER FIVE

*D*r. Steve's white truck backed up to the barn. The boots that slid out and hit the ground looked like they'd had a long, dusty day. He shook hands with Grandpa and nodded to Selah, but his eyes were only for his new patient.

"How's she been to handle, Ed?"

"She's reactive and wary, but understandable considering her circumstances."

"All you gave her was two grams of Bute?"

"That's right."

Dr. Steve stepped to the mare and let her sniff his hand before he ran his hands over her in an easy, practiced manner. His expression showed total concentration.

Through his inspection, the mare remained equally focused on the vet. She flinched and flipped her head. Her ears tipped toward him, and her eyes followed his every movement.

Flicking a light across her eye, he examined her pupils. "She is going to need some routine care wherever she ends up. You think this is the mare that broke free after the trailer wreck a couple of years ago?"

"We are just speculating at this point."

"Guess the sheriff can sort it out for you. In the meantime, I'll take care of the main issues. Let's see what we are dealing with here."

"Oh, Selah." Grandpa snapped his finger. "In the back of my truck is a bag of alfalfa cubes I picked up for Miss Katie's goats. You can use those as treats. I think she's eaten all the carrots anyway."

Selah filled an old coffee can with cubes. She stood by Grandpa and fed the mare the alfalfa cubes while the vet examined the cuts. The treats kept her interest, but she never totally took her attention off what Dr. Steve was doing to her. She tolerated him, but only barely.

"She did some damage, for sure." Dr. Steve shook his head. "The wounds need washing, antiseptic, and then ointment. Not going to put in any stitches. Pressure bandages should do the trick. Think a shot of antibiotic is appropriate, and a shot of tetanus is mandatory."

Dr. Steve talked to the horse through the process. The mare pinned her ears in warning and shifted about a great deal. Selah tried to keep the mare's horsey mind busy by keeping her mouth full. Then the mare's agitation boiled over, and she struck out with her front hooves. Only the vet's quick moves saved his knee from her assault. Grandpa's fast reaction pulled Selah out of reach of the horse's deadly weapons.

Selah stumbled backward. Her mouth gapped in shock. "What's wrong with you? Dr. Steve's trying to help you. I'm just feeding you treats. You could've hurt me."

"Didn't like that, I guess." Dr. Steve resumed his exam without reprimanding the horse. "She's a little opinionated on how she should be treated. Someone needs to work on her manners."

"Do we need to put a twitch on her, Steve?" Grandpa asked.

"Twitch?" Selah sprang in front of Grandpa. "What's a twitch?"

"It is a chain on a stick that you put over her top lip and tighten just enough to change the horse's focus."

"You can't do that! She would never trust us again, Grandpa."

"Whoever trains her will have to work that out later, Selah. Right now, the important thing is that she not hurt you or Dr. Steve while he's trying to help her."

"No! A twitch would hurt her, and she wouldn't understand."

"She's dangerous, Selah. We can't risk it. We have to put Dr. Steve's welfare above causing her temporary discomfort."

"It's okay, Ed. For now, she's all set. I got what I needed to do done. When her owner's located, they'll have to get her wormed, give her shots, and have her teeth floated."

Selah bit her lip to keep from crying like a baby. *Owner? She's mine!*

"Keep her penned up, and if she's still here, those bandages will need to be changed out in about three days," instructed Dr. Steve.

Grandpa shook Dr. Steve's hand. "We'll see what tomorrow brings. I can't thank you enough, Steve, for coming to check her out for us. We sure appreciate you. Bring your daughter around sometime to hang out with Selah while she's here."

"She'd love that, Ed. Let me know if the mare runs a fever or stops eating." Dr. Steve strode purposefully to his truck, dropped down the doors on his supply box in the bed, and slammed the truck door on his last call of the day.

Grandpa led the black mare to her paddock for the night. "If I didn't know better," he said to the mare, "I'd swear we'd met before. I can't get over feeling I should know you. You look like a smaller version of... No, it can't be. Guess I've gone crazy as I've gotten old."

"Can I give her some of this dried beet pulp, Grandpa?" Selah asked, coming up behind him.

He stirred it with his finger, but shook his head. "Best not. It looks all right, but the stuff is pretty old. Would you go up into the hayloft and get her a couple flakes from that bale of Bermuda hay? It's last year's hay that I was going to compost, but never got around to it. The color's good, and it's not moldy. If you'll do that, I will find a water bucket and get it set up."

She streaked to the loft.

He watched the mare as the water ran into the tub. Already, she had sniffed out all the corners of the paddock, hobbling from one end to the other and back again. "You are a little temperamental but still quite remarkable." He shut off the water. "I can't believe I'm saying this, but I think I may be as smitten with you as Selah. Don't you dare tell her."

Selah backed quietly away so he wouldn't know she'd overheard him. Grandpa was *smitten*! Once on the loft stairs again, she let her boots scuff on the wood. He turned to smile at her and waved her over to the paddock. "There you are. Toss the hay."

Giving approval of the hay, the horse pulled a big mouthful through the grate. Standing tall, she stared off across the pasture. Her mind absent as she chewed. Then she walked off, still with the hay hanging out of her mouth, as if she was too busy to eat and had somewhere important to go.

"Selah, your mind must be in the same place as the mare because you look as dazed as she does. Let's go to the house. We will check on her after dinner."

"The mare keeps a close eye on me. Maybe she thinks I'm an alfalfa and carrot vending machine." Selah dragged a little, following Grandpa back to the house with Skunk dragging right after her.

Grandpa fixed Skunk's dinner first. "The best dog in all of Texas gets steak tonight." He opened the can of steak bits and poured it into a pink dog bowl with tiny paw prints.

"Remember when we were shopping, Grandpa, and I found this pink bowl? You didn't want a pink bowl for your 'farm dog'. But I think all things look better in pink, and I finally convinced you."

"Ah yeah, something about needing to match your boots. Convince me? You were asking the ladies in the store if they didn't think the pink bowl was the best one. I was railroaded by a five-year-old."

"Not fair, Grandpa. I was little." Selah slipped the bowl onto the floor for Skunk and stepped back as the starving dog scarfed up the steak. "Grandma must have agreed with me that pink is the best color."

"Why do you say that?"

"Because she decorated my room in pink and cream. Something about my room makes me feel warm and loved."

His mouth smiled, but his eyes looked sad. "That's because you were loved."

Skunk finished inhaling her steak and slurped the juice off her lips.

"You should've seen Skunk, Grandpa. She knew exactly what to do to take care of the horse and not scare her. She kept the buzzards away and stayed right by my mare."

Grandpa turned sharply. "Not *your* mare, Selah. I don't mean to be harsh, but this horse is not staying here. She belongs to someone. She will be leaving as soon as the deputy notifies them she's been found."

Clouds slipped over the moon as if a child was playing with the lights of the world. One second it was dark like coal tar, and then almost bright enough to read a book. The clouds held no promise of rain, only beauty and entertainment. The whistle of the northbound train traveled crisply through the woods.

Selah sat curled up in a folding camp chair, just outside the stall but near the hay bucket. Her eyes were the only thing moving as she sucked in every detail, every movement, and every twitch of the black mare. Skunk slept soundly at the foot of the chair.

The mare stayed an easy, comfortable distance away from Selah all evening. Still, the horse's eyes, and at least one ear, remained riveted on her new little friend with cream-colored hair.

"She is watching me, thinking carrots could appear at any time."

Grandpa stared at Selah from the house and sighed. Stepping out on the porch, he tried to draw her into the house without putting his foot down too hard. "Selah, it's time for bed. Come on in now."

"Okay, Grandpa. I'm coming," Selah answered without moving. "Just a few more minutes with my dream."

From deep inside Selah, a yawn started and engulfed her whole being. With a Texas-sized exhale, she slipped from her chair onto the barn floor, where she nestled next to Skunk. Selah gathered under her head some of the hay that had filtered down from the net. The sleeping dog dreamed in the soft sand beside her. In spite of Selah's great effort, she was losing the battle to stay awake. "What should I name you? Hum... You feel like a song in my heart," she whispered as her eyes curtained.

Grandpa brought a small blanket out of the house for his sleepy girl. Selah kept her eyes closed and pretended not to hear him coming. Skunk raised her head as he approached. He rubbed under her chin, and then draped the blanket over a curled-up Selah. Selah's cat, Pearl, drifted soundlessly toward the pile of sleepers in the sand to take her rightful place next to Selah. "Sweet dreams for now, girls. I'm afraid you're in for broken hearts tomorrow."

CHAPTER SIX

Selah finished toweling off after her morning shower. Gravel crunched as a car pulled into the yard. If only the deputy had been too busy with important things to pay them a visit today—or ever.

Peeking out the window, confirmed her fears. "It's the deputy. Get away from my mare."

The deputy took a couple of pictures of the horse.

Tugging on her jeans and slipping into a shirt, she scrambled to get out there with the two men.

"Good morning, Selah. Bob, you remember my granddaughter?"

The deputy turned as she barged between him and the mare. "I hear you and ole Skunk found this horse out in the Grasslands."

"Yes, sir. We did."

"Good job. The owner has called the office every few months wondering if anyone found it. A lady up north of Athens."

Selah shuddered as if she'd been doused in ice water. "That sounds"—her teeth chattered—"like the lady is going to want her back then."

"Most definitely. The lady has been anxious about her. Went to a lot of trouble to find her in the beginning. She hired a search and rescue team to go through the Grasslands on four-wheelers. Because it is a restricted area, she had to get special permission from the National Forest Service for the four-wheelers to search it. She even had a helicopter buzz over. Of course, she kept the department on its toes about this mare too. Must be one important horse is all I can say."

Selah's heart sank. "It's not fair! *I* love her," Selah cried out as the tears gushed. She turned and ran blindly back to the house, and the screen door slammed behind her.

"Ooops," said the deputy.

She stood just inside the house with her arms crossed and peeked out at them. Her teeth clamped together so hard there was no way she could speak.

"Sorry, Ed. Guess I've done enough damage here. I'll get back to the office and call the owner."

"You couldn't know, Bob. I tried to tell her the horse couldn't stay. Yes, best get it done as fast as possible. Dragging it out will only hurt Selah more." Shaking hands, the men nodded in understanding.

With a bitter taste in her mouth, Selah watched the deputy shoehorn himself into his patrol car. The dust flew as he left her dreams in tatters.

Grandpa found her face down on her little bed in the loft. His Mary had so lovingly crafted this room for their little granddaughter. "I wish your grandma were here. She would know the right thing to say."

Sobs shook Selah's small frame. Pain contorted her face. Grandpa was helpless to comfort her.

He sat beside her and rubbed her back. "I'm sorry, honey. I do understand how much this hurts," was all he offered her. He rose from the bed and pulled the door shut behind him.

Selah rolled over. She didn't know how long she had been asleep. Her eyes felt puffy and swollen, like someone had punched her out. "Ugh... don't wake up." She lay still and took a deep breath, holding it for as long as she could, and then exhaled through her mouth. "Peace of Christ," she repeated to herself.

"I hate this. I found the mare, and I saved her. She should be mine." Looking in the mirror, she put her chin up and struggled to smile. "Mom said if you put a smile on your face, it will find its way to your heart. But Grandpa is right—some things just hurt." Selah finished her little pep talk and reached for the phone.

"Hi, Mom."

"Selah, I thought you were going to call yesterday morning. Your brothers were disappointed not to get to talk to you. Everything okay there with you and Grandpa?"

"Well, yes and no. We found a lost horse in the Grasslands. Her legs were wrapped in wire, and she was down. The buzzards wanted to eat her. Skunk watched over her while I ran home to get wire cutters. It took a long time, but we got her free and walked her to the farm. Grandpa called the deputy, who is calling the owner to come and get her. She's so beautiful, Mom. I just can't let them take her. I want to keep her in the worst way."

"Oh dear. That's gotta hurt. Wish I knew what to say, honey. Wrap your arms around yourself because I'm sending you a hug. Do you want us to come tomorrow? We miss you and would love to see you. Maybe two weeks is too long for you to be gone."

"I miss everybody too, but it's okay. I'm just sad because I know the mare will be leaving soon. She is perfect, Mom. She's the horse in my dreams. Grandpa's sad too, and I don't understand why he wants the horse to leave. He loves her. When he didn't know I was behind him, he told her he was smitten with her."

"Selah, Grandpa has his reasons. Let it go. Let's talk in the morning. Love you lots."

"Love ya back. Bye."

Selah felt better after talking to her mom. Her smile came easier now, and she headed down to see what was happening in the kitchen.

Lunch was happening. Grandpa worked intently on building his "grilled cheese grands". He'd piled on all Selah's favorites. Thick slices of Mozzarella cheese, juicy tomato, topped with bacon, topped with avocado, and more cheese.

She brought a big smile when she came into the kitchen because a plan was already hatching behind her blue eyes. A plan to see if the owner would sell the mare. What seemed an innocent smile was contagious, and soon he was smiling broadly too.

Selah fixed chocolate milk for them, and they carried lunch out to the deck. They held hands and bowed their heads while Grandpa thanked God for their food.

"Grandpa, don't you miss having the horses around? I mean, even if you didn't ride or work with 'em, you could get a 'rescue' horse."

He tilted his head thoughtfully. "Sometimes." He pushed his chair back and propped one boot up on another chair. "Sometimes," he repeated. "I've been thinking. Would you like to learn more about horses, Selah?"

She looked over at the paddocks, and her eyes riveted on the mare. Selah watched her sleep, her head drifting lower to the ground. "Oh, Grandpa, that would mean soooo much to me." While she liked what she was finally hearing from Grandpa, the horse she wanted was already here, and she wanted to keep it that way.

Grandpa swished a fly from his plate, rose from the chair, and went inside. "We can explore that," he said over his shoulder.

An excitement built inside her, and the smile on her face welled up all the way up from her toes. Finally, progress with Grandpa! This might be a good time to talk to him about asking the lady if she would sell the horse.

When he came back out to the deck, he brought a stack of books and put them in front of a grinning Selah. "You've got work to do. There's a lot to know about horses."

She sifted through the books—a small collection that identified themselves on the covers as natural horsemanship techniques. Picking up the first one, she read the author's inscription. "To Ed. Put your heart in your hand and touch the horse with love. Best of luck. Pat."

Selah's eyes darted across at Grandpa, but she didn't say anything. She picked up the next book. "To Ed. Keep it light. Dennis." The next one: "To Ed. The real deal. Stay with the method. Cooper."

"Grandpa? You know all these trainers?"

"Yes. Worked with most of them through the years. Learned something from each one."

She stood and gathered the books she'd spread across the table. When the phone rang, she asked, "Want me to get it?"

"Nah, I'll get it. Work on your lunch. I've been expecting Deputy Bob to call with news of the owner."

"The deputy?" Leaving her lunch, Selah tiptoed behind him.

"Hello?" Grandpa punched on the speakerphone.

"Ed…" A long, quiet pause followed the soft feminine voice over the wires. "This is Laura."

"Laura. It's been a while, but it's nice to hear from you."

"I'm sorry it's been so long." Laura paused. "I still miss Mary so much. So many things come up in my life that I would've shared only with her. It never seems to get any easier, knowing I can't pick up the phone and call her."

"Yeah, I know. So what's on your mind, Laura?"

"The deputy called me today and gave me your name. He had no idea we were old friends. My barn manager was driving the rig on the highway when it jackknifed. And…the reason I'm calling is the mare you found… she's Harmony's last filly." The last few words came out in a rush before Laura broke into tears. "I'm sorry I never told you, but I didn't want you to hurt anymore. I tried so hard to find the filly. It broke my heart when we couldn't."

Selah eased the rest of the way into the room as he disconnected the call. The tears streamed down Grandpa's cheeks as he gazed over his empty pastures. He turned and saw her. "The mare…" He faltered. "The black mare you found is Harmony's last foal. Her name is Mary's… Mary's Dream Song." He gave a strangled cough and tapped his chest with a balled-up fist. "I'm going for a walk."

Selah stood in stunned disbelief. The little black mare in the paddock was the daughter of her grandmother's dressage horse? But the mare in the video was tall and long legged. The mare outside was only 14.3 hands high.

Selah hurried to Grandpa's office and pushed the old tape into the player. Rewinding it to the freestyle test, she studied the horse. She had such an air of superiority, but with a gentleness of heart. In that instant, she made the connection between mother and daughter. The same proud, confident, almost defiant, spirit lit the eyes of both horses.

Stopping the player, Selah felt pulled to the paddock. She'd spent every waking minute hanging out in the barn admiring the mare, usually with Pearl cuddled in her lap.

Grandpa beat her there. Leaning against the top railing, he said, "Guess you can have your wish. If I hunted the whole state of Texas, I doubt I could find a better horse for you. If she has her mother's heart, which it looks like she does, then she will be a one-girl horse. She'll work the best for you and give everyone else a half-hearted effort, if she even gives them the time of day." Grandpa got quiet, and his eyes followed the mare's movements. "We have our work cut out for us. If she is anything like her mother, she'll keep us on our toes."

"The lady doesn't want the horse back?" Turning to look into his brown eyes, Selah asked, "Is this for real Grandpa?"

"The 'lady' was your grandmother's dearest friend, and she said it would give her great joy for you to have the mare. Laura wants to come see both of you soon."

"It's like—she is the perfect gift from my grandma," Selah whispered.

Grandpa couldn't say anything at all.

Life was crazy—different. And now, all about her horse. Everything Selah hoped and dreamed of, for as long as she could remember, stood in front of her this minute. She perched on a fence board next to him, extending an orange gift. The mare lengthened her neck for the carrot, but kept her body well out of reach.

"We need to decide on a name for you. We can't just keep calling you 'horse.' If only you could tell me what you like. Your registered name, Mary's Dream Song, is beautiful." Selah let the name roll off her tongue to get a feel for it.

"You're a song in my heart. But you're also a dream come true. I'm thinkin' you were perfectly named when you were born, and we should stick with it. For short, you could be Dream."

Carrot devoured, the mare let Selah scratch lightly right under her jawbone. After a minute, the mare closed her eyes and leaned into the rub. "It must feel odd to her to be penned up when she has been free for so long. She almost looks like she is having a sweet dream. Oh, Grandpa, she is my sweet dream, and I think that's what we should call her."

"I like that, Selah. Your grandmother would like it too," he said with a smile.

"I'm sorry I don't remember more about Grandma."

"You were only four, sunshine, but she loved you with everything in her. She would be ecstatic that you and Sweet Dream are together."

"I know she did, Grandpa. I can feel it in the room that she decorated for me. And I hope she feels my joy. Joy!" Selah squealed, extending both arms in the air. "Joy!" She twirled around and around with her arms flung back. "Joy! Crazy joy! What a perfect, glorious day."

Grandpa smiled at her display of childish bliss. "I'm gonna get my camera. Be back in a minute."

A sharp tug on her jeans yanked Selah off balance. As she whirled around, Dream snapped her head back between the fence boards. The mare arched her neck and flipped her nose up and down. Selah's pocket from her jeans dangled from Sweet Dream's teeth.

Gasping, Selah covered the new ventilation in her jeans with her hand. "Grrr... Gimme that before Grandpa sees you."

CHAPTER SEVEN

*I*n a heartbeat, the farm became a bustling place. Calls to make, tack to clean, hay and feed to put up, and a horse to care for. "We need to get busy around here." Grandpa put his arm around Selah's shoulders, and they walked to a room in the barn that hadn't been opened in a while—the tack room. Grime and cobwebs hung thick.

"I'm not going in there, Grandpa. Those spiders are so big they could carry me away and feed me to their babies."

"You're not going to turn into a city girl on me, are ya?"

"Nothing could make me go in there—nothing. It's grodie."

He looked at the memories hanging on the wall. "I'd rather not go in there either." Pictures of Grandma with Harmony covered one wall, and horse show ribbons plastered what wasn't covered in pictures. From the wall hooks, he pulled a training rope halter, a long lead, and a long white stick with a tightly woven cord tied to it. "The saddle over there will fit you." He pointed into a cluttered corner.

"We'll need to check the fittings, clean and oil it. There's plenty of time for that, because you'll be working her in the round pen before you can ride her."

Tugging the heavy old door shut with a heave, he deposited the stuff from the tack room onto his workbench to clean up later. He wiped the years of dust off the notepad and wrote on his barn To Do list: fix tack room door and purge tack room. "We should call Dr. Steve and ask him to come back out. She needs her shots, and he can evaluate her soundness."

Grandpa slid his keys from his pocket. "In the meantime, if you will spend as much time as you can where she can see you, that will help. She needs to learn that she doesn't get hay unless you feed her."

"Twist my arm."

"Such a funny girl today. Anyway, because she needs to learn good things come from you, I've purposely only put a gallon of water in her bucket this morning. I want to turn that chore over to you. Keep an eye on it, but don't refill it right away. Let her get a little thirsty. Then let the water trickle into her bucket and stand there while she drinks. When she stops, you stop. That will keep her focused on you. Will that keep you busy while I go to town to get hay?"

Selah's smile stretched all the way across her face. "It will." She ran to gather things she would need for her stakeout by Sweet Dream. Settling in, she waved to Grandpa as the truck moved out. She stacked and restacked the training books, finding it hard to choose which one to start with today.

Book in one hand and hay in the other, she put only a little hay into the net at a time, and she sat as close as possible. If the mare made an effort to engage her, Selah rewarded her with an alfalfa cube.

"Sweet Dream, will you be my best friend? We are meant for each other, just like your mother and my grandma. Just imagine the adventures we can have together."

Selah looked up from the training manual and watched Dream hobble around the paddock. Since the mare hadn't come into the stall for a bite of hay in a while now, Selah unlatched the door and eased into the stall.

"Dream, I have a carrot for you." Dream walked to Selah and snapped the carrot from her hand. Selah reached out to touch Dream's shoulder. At her touch, Dream's ears snapped back as she wheeled sharply and bolted from the stall into the paddock. Her hip slammed into Selah and threw her up against the wall. With the breath knocked out of her, Selah slid down the wall to the stall floor. Dream's hooves sprayed shavings all over her, and for a moment, she couldn't see anything. "Breathe… breathe… Grandpa is going to be furious."

Dream's face appeared again in the doorway. Her head was low, and her nose jutted toward Selah.

"Did you come back to finish the job?" Dream inched forward, sucked back, and inched forward again. "Or are you trying to say you're sorry? Best friends don't act like that, Dream." She pulled herself to her feet, tugging on a wood splinter in the palm of her hand. She backed out of the stall, keeping a close eye on her wild thing, and kept pressure on the new bloody hole in her hand. A little dazed, she sank into the chair, sucked on her splinter wound, and rubbed her sore shoulder. "He told me to keep a fence between us. I should've listened. If he finds out what you did, he'll give you back to Miss Laura." She brushed the stall bedding off her clothes and shook it from her short hair.

51

The afternoon seemed to flash by and disappear into thin air. Soon Grandpa was back with his truck bed loaded with beautiful, fragrant hay, and another big bag of alfalfa cubes.

"How are you two getting along?" he asked.

"She is doing fine about coming up to the hay net to get a bite. Then she will take her bite of hay and move away from me. She got a drink once, and I did what you told me. I stood as near as I could to the bucket and slowly let water flow into it for her. She didn't move off right away."

"That sounds good."

"She is happy to take an alfalfa cube from my hand, but if I reach out to touch her shoulder, she flies to get away from me." Best to leave out the part about her being on the wrong side of the fence.

"She is wary. Perfectly natural, considering she thinks she is wild. You keep at it because it'll dawn on her soon that you are the source of all good things for her. Until then, be extra careful around her."

Selah looked at him and kept her mouth shut.

"You may think this strange, but her injury works to your advantage."

"How could there be anything good about Dream being hurt?"

"When King David was a shepherd boy, if a sheep in the flock didn't stay with the shepherd, he'd have to break its leg."

"Ahhck..." Selah sucked in her breath.

"He'd carry that sheep on his shoulders everywhere until it healed. By then, the sheep trusted and looked to the shepherd for its care."

"That's just mean."

"If the sheep was left to its own devices, it would've gotten eaten by the wolves. They have to learn to stay with the shepherd and the herd."

"Oh, so while it hurt, that's better than dead?"

"Yeah, better than dead."

"Let me guess…. That's a Bible story, and the moral of the story is?"

"Yes, yes it is. The Shepherd with his sheep is a picture for us about how we should stay near to our heavenly Father. This mare is mostly wild, and she needs to learn to trust you. She is hurting right now, and if she looks to you to take care of her when she is helpless, then she's going to see you as her best friend."

Helpless? Yeah, right, she wanted to say. Instead, she said, "Best friends forever."

He smiled. "Dr. Steve was at the feed store. He's gonna come out first thing in the morning and check her out for us. I'm guessing she'll check out all right, and we'll be able to work her in the round pen soon."

"I'd better finish *Round Penning Basics*."

"What've you been doing with your time?"

She made a face at him.

"I've got a DVD for round penning. We could watch it tonight," he suggested as they walked to the house.

She raised her eyebrows and popped her eyes wide. "Yeah." She dragged the TV trays into the living room while he cooked up some dinner.

Grandpa stirred the noodles into the pot of hamburger and tomatoes. He watched the black mare out the window, "What a wonder you are. It feels like nothing less than a miracle to have you find your way to my farm. But will I ever look at you and not feel the pain your mother caused me?"

CHAPTER EIGHT

*G*randpa handed Selah the remote. "Stop it whenever you
need to." A stout black colt with a spotted rump, pivoting
its head from side to side, filled the screen. Dakota was trotting
nervously in a round pen, his energy as high as his head. He
snapped his knees up and flung his hooves forward. The trainer
stood in the center talking to the camera, ignoring the horse.
Cooper explained the horse's actions and how he knew Dakota
was processing his dilemmas. He said that the signals the horse
sent revealed his state of mind. The horse's body position, the
way he held his head, where his ears focused were all important
to Cooper.

Intent on the round-penning lesson, Selah leaned forward
with both hands holding the remote. The trainer held one arm
up and pointed his finger in the direction he wanted the horse
to go. When the young horse turned toward Cooper, reared, and
stomped the ground with one foot, Cooper ran at him, pointing

to give direction. With his other arm, he swung a stick with a cord tied on the end of it. Dakota took off as fast as he could go in a circle. Tiring, the horse stopped, tucked its tail, and spun his hindquarters toward Cooper.

"Uh-oh. It's going to kick. Dakota's in trouble now."

Cooper made the horse's feet move faster to correct Dakota's show of disrespect. The Appaloosa horse got the message and scooted to obey.

"How amazing the horse knows to go where the trainer points."

After several more turns, the horse started to relax and lowered his head. This time when Cooper backed up from the horse and pointed in the opposite direction, he had the horse's attention. The colt turned to look at Cooper for an instant, and then moved off in the new direction.

"Did you see that, Grandpa? Super wow." She never took her eyes off the screen. "I so want to be able to do that with Sweet Dream."

Grandpa yawned.

After a few more minutes, the trainer backed up and put one hand up in front of his face, wiggling his finger as if to call a small child. Dakota pivoted and trotted right to the trainer and stopped in front of him. Cooper rubbed the horse's black face with the stick and rewarded Dakota by letting him rest.

"Now that is just amazing. Did I say that already?"

"Only about ten times."

"It looks so fun! I never imagined you could play games with a horse."

"Oh, you keep watching. It gets better."

The trainer threw the lead rope over the horse's back, under his belly, and around his legs. The horse stood still, looking relaxed and quiet. When Cooper brought out a plastic bag and attached it to his stick, Selah stared in wide-eyed astonishment, as did Dakota.

"Anything that moves and makes a noise will startle a horse," Grandpa explained.

The horse woke up, snorted, and leaped sideways. Dakota swung his head, and a flash of white teeth snapped toward Cooper's arm. The trainer blocked the attack with a well-placed elbow. Soon, Dakota stopped and cocked his head to look at and reconsider the bag. Then he did what Cooper called "licking his brain", which was actually licking his lips.

"I know what that means. The horse is thinking."

The trainer took the bag away, rubbed the colt, and let it rest while he explained to his video audience what he was doing and why.

"Grandpa?" Selah paused the video. "I don't get how the horse knows when the trainer wants him to stand still or when the trainer wants him to move away. It looks like the same bag waving to me."

"Observant question, Selah. I'd say it's body language—pressure. If the trainer looks relaxed and turns away, the horse knows he doesn't have to move. If the trainer is standing tall, leaning in, and looking intently at the horse, then it knows it's being told to move its feet."

"Forward, backward, side to side?"

"You're getting the idea."

She smiled, mentally patted herself on the back, and turned the video back on. He yawned again, pushed back in his recliner, and popped up the footrest. Moonlight inched across the floor, and the video played on. No way could she sleep when she had so much to learn. Unlike Grandpa, who slept quite well in his chair. Twenty minutes later, she dragged her weary body to the couch and snuggled into the soft pillows with her eyes glued to the horse in the round pen. When her eyes grew heavy, she dropped into darkness. *Who am I kidding? I can't train a horse—any horse—let along a wild one.*

CHAPTER NINE

A small glass of fresh orange juice appeared on the TV tray beside Selah. The TV was dark. The doubts that pushed their way into her mind last night ran through her head again as the OJ slid down her throat. Then she remembered she had a responsibility outside, scrambled to her feet, and hurried through the house.

Grandpa stood at the stove. "Good morning."

"Be right back. I have to take care of Dream."

Sweet Dream stood close to the feed bucket with her eyes riveted on the door of the house. A nicker, so soft Selah could barely hear it, greeted her. The mare's dark eyes followed Selah to the feed room. Her hooves shuffled along the stall wallboards in anticipation of the hay about to hit her net. Before the hay even dropped, the mare grabbed for it.

"Somebody's hungry." Selah checked the water bucket. "And thirsty too. You drank it all up." When the mare finished the little bit of hay, she'd want more water. "I'll wait on you." Selah leaned on the top rail, watching her dream eat hay. "I can hardly believe you're here. I have a horse." A satisfied smile rested on her face. "And I forgive you for yesterday, and the day before yesterday, and the day before. I mess up over and over again too." She positioned herself close to the bucket. If the mare wanted water, she'd have to overcome being uncomfortable with Selah to get it.

The mare finished her hay and inched closer.

Selah let the water dribble into the bucket. Dream drank her fill, and Selah turned the water off again. Reaching her hand out, she rubbed Sweet Dream's face between her eyes. The horse accepted the face rub without a fuss. A victory! "I will win your heart, Sweet Dream, and I will work hard and learn how to train you." She hurried back to the house. "Grandpa, she let me rub her face."

"Good progress. Hungry?" He pushed a plate of eggs in her direction. "I have something I want to share with you. It's an equestrian team near and dear to the hearts of Texas. They won a reining competition, years back. The only team ever to ride and win bareback and without a bridle."

"No way?"

"Yes way. We can watch it after breakfast. It's a short clip stored on VideoTube."

Selah's pancakes disappeared in record time. As she put her dish in the sink, he slipped a silver belt buckle into his pocket. Before she could ask him about it, the video announcer reverently said, "Mary and Illusion."

The horse and rider stepped into the hushed arena. The audience collectively held their breath. The rider caressed the horse's neck. Hand over hand, she stroked the horse's mane in a beautiful, rhythmic, soothing motion. The horse lifted in the front as if to fly like a Pegasus, but instead, they transitioned into a carousel horse canter.

"Ahhhh. I've never seen anything so beautiful." The announcer spoke in a hushed tone.

The horse and rider performed a pattern of circles at different speeds and varying diameters, with a lead change precisely at the midpoint. The pair halted sharply in the immediate center of the pattern.

"Wow. They are awesome." Selah's mouth gaped wide.

Grandpa's eyes were riveted on Selah as she watched the magic on the screen. He choked up as he tried to say, "They're not done."

In that instant, they spun like a game wheel, first one way, and then another. To finish, the pair galloped hard to one end of the arena. The horse stopped running forward and froze in form, causing it to slide. It looked as if the horse was about to sit down on its rump. It was so near the ground, its tail swept the dirt. They floated gracefully. They could've been going down a snowy slope on skis except what flew into the air was dirt, instead of white powder.

The audience on the video went absolutely wild, and so did Selah. "Wow! Oh wow! Did you see that? Oh, Grandpa, can you teach me to do that?" She stopped. *Is that a tear in Grandpa's eye? He'll be embarrassed if I ask.* "They take your breath away, don't they, Grandpa? You can't even tell she is asking the horse to do any of that."

"She was a very special, gifted young woman."

"I want to be like her when I grow up."

"I am hoping you will be like her too. That's your grandmother, Selah. I fell in love with her on that day."

"Come. We have work to do." Grandpa swung the door to the tack room open wide and tried to usher Selah inside.

"I'm not going in there. I told you, Grandpa. I'm not a fan of spiders."

"Look."

She peered tentatively inside. Where did the cobwebs go? And the last eight years of grime? "Amazing."

"It's amazing what I can get done while you sleep the day away."

She smacked his arm and puckered her mouth at him. "I did not."

"Here's your rag and saddle soap." They worked on cleaning the halter, leads, and things from storage. Skunk tucked herself right behind them at the workbench. If they tried to do anything fun without her, Skunk would know it.

"So after you saw her ride, what did you do? How did you meet her?"

"I tried to get close enough to meet her, but the crowd mobbed her after the ride. Then two weeks later, she did a demonstration ride at an expo I was at in Tennessee. After the demo, she gave credit to the Lord for her talents, and I knew I'd marry her if only I could meet her. As it turned out, she had a weakness for funnel cakes. We never went to an event again without sharing a funnel cake."

"That's sweet, Grandpa."

"You're her granddaughter in every way. Use the talents the good Lord gave you and work hard. There isn't anything you can't do when you pursue your passion."

"Yeah, right. I wish I believed that. Grandma was amazing, but I'm not."

CHAPTER TEN

Sweet Dream stood at the far end of her paddock looking out over the pasture. Pearl meandered along the fence under the horse's nose. Noses touched, and new friends were made. Pearl arched her back and rubbed on the nearest fencepost to seal the deal. Sweet Dream went back to gazing at the grass on the other side of the fence.

Dr. Steve's white truck drove into the farmyard with a quick honk to announce his arrival. Callie, the vet tech, eased out of the truck and busied herself gathering supplies. Dr. Steve opened his door but stayed seated in the truck. He was deep in conversation with someone. From the furrow in his brow, it looked like they were having a horse-problem day. Dropping his phone onto the seat of the truck, he climbed out ready for duty.

Grandpa threw a rope around Sweet Dream's neck to catch her for Dr. Steve's examination. Sweet Dream resisted the stress of being rushed and refused to come out of the paddock. The mare pulled back, reared, and shook her black head.

Grandpa leaped to the side as she struck at him with her hooves. He snapped the rope and jerked her off balance. Sweet Dream spun to face him and snorted rebellion.

Selah wanted to rush to Sweet Dream and calm her. The wild look in the mare's eyes kept Selah back. *You're not wild anymore, Dream. You need to stop acting wild before Grandpa decides you're too dangerous for me.*

"Take your time with her, Ed," Dr. Steve called, pushing his sunglasses up to nest them in his thick brown hair. "Wow. Things changed in a heartbeat around here. You save a lost horse which shockingly turns into being your own horse." Dr. Steve shook his head in amazement.

"You'll get no argument from us on that one, Doc."

"Well, let's have a look at those wounds. What's her name?"

"She is my Sweet Dream."

"Perfect." Dr. Steve nodded. "Callie here is going to remove the bandages, and then we will check her soundness." Turning to Callie, he warned, "Watch this mare, Callie. She has a wicked left hook." He slipped his stethoscope from around his neck and inserted the earpieces. "She walked out of the stall today better than when I first saw her. Some rest and TLC have been good for her."

Grandpa said, "She hobbled around the paddock the first day and steadily improved since then."

"You want her to get all her vaccinations today too, right?"

"Yes. Thought we'd go ahead with that, though I haven't decided if she is a keeper yet."

"I heard the story in town about her being one of Harmony's colts." Dr. Steve moved deftly around the mare. "It's eerie, that a colt from Mary's horse would find her way here." He listened to her heart, lungs, and for gut sounds. His hands went over her, searching for anything that might be a problem. Stooping over, he worked his way down each leg, inch by inch, looking for issues. The mare struggled and pulled away as he lifted each front hoof off the ground. When he tried to lift a back hoof, she lashed at him with it as quick as a rattler. "Never mind," he said.

"Sorry, Doc," Grandpa said. "If we keep her, we'll work on that."

"That'd be good. Selah, it looks like all you need to do is keep some cream on the wounds so the hair will grow back."

Dream's black ears flattened against her head as he administered her shots. She squealed and kicked out at Dr. Steve with her hind leg. Her nose flipped up and down like a nervous twitch. One front hoof repeatedly struck on the ground.

Selah backed away while sending a telepathic message to Dream. *Behave yourself, Dream. Grandpa is watching you.*

Dr. Steve picked up his clipboard and jotted down his notes. "Callie, would you get a Power Pack out of the truck, please." Turning to Selah, he said, "She has a lot of worms—you can feel them under her skin. Horses pick those up while grazing. They look like her biggest health issue, though she certainly has behavioral issues. Follow the directions on the pack Callie gives you."

Selah bit the inside of her cheek as she concentrated. She wanted to know everything about taking care of "her" horse.

Callie passed the Power Pack to Selah and took the lead line back from Grandpa. The moment of truth. *Is Dream lame? Or is she ready to train?* Callie walked the mare out to a level, solid area. The pair marched back and forth while Dr. Steve analyzed Dream's movements.

"Trot her, please, Callie."

Everyone studied the mare as she trotted alongside Callie. Selah tried not to let her imagination get the best of her, but the mare's head bobbed a little when she trotted. Was she tender in the front? Or was it the rear? Was it serious?

"She looks better," Dr. Steve concluded. "She does still have a little something going on in the right front. Just keep an eye on it. I think she will be fine."

Selah asked, in her best grown-up voice, "Can she be turned loose in the pasture yet, Dr. Steve?" In her head, she was screeching, "My mare is going to be all right. We will go on rides and adventures together. We will be soul mates just like my grandma and Illusion."

"Sure, she can handle it now unless she runs around too fast and is in danger of falling. I think she's way smarter than that."

"She'd have to be," Grandpa agreed. "She survived on her own for two years."

Delighted with the mare's checkup, Selah's bliss bubbled from her mouth. "Thank you. Thank you. Isn't she wonderful? She's so pretty! Don't you think she's pretty?"

"Nothing better for a girl's heart than a horse, is there, Ed?"

"God is good," Grandpa agreed.

Dr. Steve lowered his voice. "God's been good to the horse, bringing her here. Not so sure how it'll work out for Selah. She's a cantankerous little mare."

CHAPTER ELEVEN

A young lady with a notepad and a camera eased out of a tiny, cobalt blue electric car. Coming toward Grandpa, she held her hand out. "Hi, I'm Nancy Glenn. I'm with the *Canaan Item*. I wondered if I might talk to you about a horse you found."

"How did you hear that?"

"It's my job." Nancy laughed. "I'd like to do a feature article on your granddaughter and the horse, if it's okay."

Grandpa took her extended hand. "Hello. I'm Ed, and this young lady is my granddaughter, Selah." Stepping back, he scratched his head. "Selah, what do you think?"

"Dream and I will be famous. How fun is that?"

"I guess it's okay with us, but we will have to ask Selah's parents."

"Yes, sir, I understand."

"Be back in a few minutes. Selah, why don't you introduce Miss Glenn to Dream?"

Selah pointed proudly to the treasure in the paddock. "Isn't she beautiful?"

"She has a friendly face," Nancy reported.

Humph, Selah rolled her eyes, *if you only knew.* "Looks can be deceiving." The mare looked wide-eyed at them. Selah was sure the mare was wondering, *What now?*

Grandpa rejoined them at the fence. "Selah's parents say it's okay if you disable something on your camera that would identify Selah's location. I don't know what she's talking about, but she said you'd know."

"No worries. I will be using a regular camera and not something allowing GPS enabling."

"I'm glad you made sense out of that." He gestured for them to move to the porch.

Nancy perched on the edge of the chair and crossed her ankles. Selah attempted to sit in the chair like Nancy. But her boots didn't cross with the same effect as Nancy's city shoes, so she gave it up.

"This is so —so beautiful," Nancy said. "I would love to live on a farm like this except I think I'd hate mowing all this pasture more than I love the country. Do you get to spend much time here, Selah?"

"I'd live here if I could. I have to talk Grandpa into coming to get me to come for a weekend. In the summer, I get to spend two weeks here."

"Quite an adventure you've had on this visit. Can you tell me about finding the horse?"

She nodded. "Skunk and I were out in the Grasslands reading—"

"Skunk?"

"Oh yes," Selah said, with a little giggle. "Skunk is Grandpa's dog. Davy, my little brother, named her. When he saw her as a puppy, he thought the white streak on her black head meant she was a skunk."

Looking over at Skunk asleep on the porch, Nancy chuckled. "Such a pretty dog to be called Skunk."

"Oh, she doesn't mind at all. Anyway, we were coming in, and I thought I saw something way off in the field. You couldn't tell anything was there until she moved. I climbed a tree to see her better. She threw up her head and looked around like something was after her. All of a sudden, she was running a million miles an hour."

"Was something chasing her?"

"Not that I could tell. She may have heard me smacking into the tree trunk. I nearly fell out of the tree when I lost my balance. Anyway, she disappeared in a flash, and I stood in the tree, not really sure I'd seen a horse at all."

Bringing drinks, Grandpa asked, "What do you mean—'you almost fell out of a tree'? You didn't tell me that part." He handed some sweet tea to Nancy, pulled up another chair, and held Selah's drink in her direction. His eyes narrowed. "What do you mean you almost fell out of a tree?"

Selah reached for her drink, only Grandpa wouldn't let go of it. "Almost, but I didn't."

He released the drink. "Anything else you should tell me?"

She squirmed in her chair and stuck the straw in her mouth. *Not that I dare tell you.*

As the quiet lengthened, Nancy asked, "So, what happened next?"

Relieved to have the focus shift, Selah continued, "Grandpa went to town the next day and talked to the men at the barbershop.

Al, the owner, knew about a horse trailer that jackknifed about two years ago. He told Grandpa the horse in transport got loose and they never found it."

"I heard in town that the horse had been stolen."

"No! We didn't steal her! I found her, and Grandpa called the deputy."

"I mean, I heard she'd been stolen from her farm when the wreck happened."

"That's not true." Selah sighed and continued, "I wanted to go out the next day, but the thunderstorms were huge. The day after that, Grandpa had an appointment, and he said we should turn it over to the sheriff. I couldn't wait. I needed to go right then. Skunk and I had gone almost two miles before we found her."

"And she let you catch her?"

"Oh no, not at all. We found her because a big flock of buzzards was flying over her. She was trapped in wire."

"You must have been terrified."

"Yes, ma'am, I was. Skunk and I scared them off, but the horse couldn't get up. I left Skunk on guard and came home to get wire cutters. Grandpa was home by then, so he came with me."

"Was she hurt?"

"She had cuts on her legs, so she was limping."

"I heard in town that it got more interesting real fast, didn't it?"

"Yes, ma'am, it did. The deputy came out and took some pictures of Dream so he could e-mail them to the person who lost her. The owner turned out to be an old friend of Grandpa's. Sweet Dream is a foal from my grandmother's horse that Grandpa had given to Grandma's best friend when my grandma died."

"Oh, that sounds like a God-incidence. And so you get to keep her?"

"Oh, yes, ma'am," Selah said, with great enthusiasm. "She is mine, and I am hers. We are meant to be. It's like she is a special gift from my grandma."

"Ah, how dear is that?" Nancy smiled.

"Actually," Grandpa interjected, "the jury is still out on if she can stay."

Selah's heart seized up.

"The mare is pretty wild, so it's hard to tell much about her personality right now. If her disposition turns out unsuitable for Selah, then the mare will be returned to my wife's old friend, Laura."

Selah's face tightened as she bit the inside of her cheek. Inside her head, she screamed at Grandpa, *You can't send my Dream away.*

As Selah fought back the tears, her cat Pearl gracefully sauntered into the center of attention. Cream-colored hair embedded itself in Nancy's black slacks as Pearl welcomed Nancy to her territory. Nancy reached down and stroked Pearl. "Oh my, she is soft. What a lovely kitty. Her fur is the same color as your hair, Selah."

"This is Pearl. I call her our walking fur dispenser." Selah scooped up the cat. "She is my best, best friend. She was the tiny one in the litter and the only cream color. Pearl is an 'ornament' around the farm. She is feminine decoration only and sees no reason to perform any catlike duties."

Selah knew Grandpa wouldn't be able to resist.

"She is worthless as a farm cat," he said, heading into the house.

"Well, she is divine. What is next for you and Sweet Dream?"

"Grandpa and I are going to train her. I want to teach her tricks, and he's going to teach me to ride like my grandma. She rode her horse, Illusion, without a saddle or bridle."

"I'm impressed, Selah. Quite a story. I'm excited you shared it with me, and I'm sure my readers will love it. May I get some pictures?"

"I'll get Grandpa to catch Sweet Dream." She chased into the house after him.

Grandpa posed the mare, and Selah stood nearby, but not too near. Skunk sat smartly in front where the little ham tilted her head for the camera as if she was modeling an Easter bonnet.

"Thank you so much. You are going to love the story when it's done."

Selah looked at Grandpa as he watched Miss Nancy wave and drive off. *My mare's not going anywhere, Grandpa!*

CHAPTER TWELVE

*T*raining videos and books filled Selah's next few days. "When Dream is ready, I will be ready too." When she wasn't studying, she helped Grandpa check and repair the fence line. For now, the mare could use the one acre adjacent to the paddock. They tied open the paddock gate so Sweet Dream could be in the paddock or graze in the pasture.

"With the water and hay still in the stall, Sweet Dream will be coming into the barn after it so we can interact with her a lot," Grandpa said.

Sweet Dream walked and trotted around her new space, checking it out. Selah watched to make sure she didn't try to do anything stupid like jump the fence and escape. "Please, God, don't let her jump out and get away."

"I still want you to keep a fence between the two of you, Selah. She is wild, and you can't forget it for a minute. You saw how fast she defended herself using her front hooves on Dr. Steve."

"She just got here, and she was scared. She likes me."

"She likes your carrots." Grandpa put his arm around her shoulder and turned her to face the horse. "She can stand there looking like some old gray mare, but if you trust her before she respects you, she will hurt you. Her wildness and her instinct to survive make her unpredictable and dangerous."

"She wouldn't hurt me." *Not on purpose.*

"Don't you believe it. We'll know a whole lot more about how much she can be trusted after we start her in the round pen."

"Don't you think we're ready?" Selah tugged on his shirtsleeve and stutter nodded.

"Yes, I do think both of you are ready. The mare doesn't look at all sore. She is moving freely and easily. Would you like to start Sweet Dream in the round pen in the morning?"

"A hundred times yes. And I have a surprise for you, Grandpa. Sweet Dream and I have been working on something," She took him by the hand and led him toward the barn.

Sweet Dream was in the middle of the pasture with her nose buried in the grass. Selah lifted her voice and called to the mare. "Dream."

The mare's head shot up, and she spun toward the sound.

"Dream!" Selah called again.

At that, the mare walked straight toward Selah, her head held high and her focus intent. About thirty feet away, she broke into a trot and closed the distance between them. The mare stopped and stretched out her soft nose toward Selah. Barely able to reach, she lipped the carrot in Selah's hand, drawing it into her mouth.

"Will ya look at that?" Grandpa said.

"Isn't she the greatest? I told you she liked me. I can't describe what it does to my heart when she runs to me when I call her— but it feels amazing!"

"That's rare and special. It's nice to see her being more respectful. You have a way with her, Selah."

"I want to teach her all kinds of tricks."

He grinned. "I have a feeling she is going to teach you all kinds of tricks. Come on. Let's go play horse in the round pen."

Selah liked the sound of that and skipped behind him up the little hill. Her training was about to begin.

"Okay, you are the trainer, and I am the horse," he said. "From the video, what is the first thing you do?"

"Establish direction."

"Yes, next?"

"Cluck if she doesn't go. If she still doesn't go, swing the training stick."

"Very good. This exercise forces you to think through problems you're likely to have when you start with Dream. It will also help you to get comfortable with your training tools. Now try it."

Grandpa did a great imitation of a horse that didn't have a clue what was going on. Everything she asked him to do, he did the opposite. Selah practiced sending Grandpa out to the rail. She told him to go faster, turn, head in the other direction, and stop. "I think I get it, Grandpa. I hope Sweet Dream gets it."

"I'm going to need a lawn chair up here," he said laughing. "You're making me lose weight."

"You're a stubborn horse, Grandpa. Mr. Cooper would call you fat and lazy."

"We'll just see if you can get Skunk to volunteer to be your practice horse for your next training session. Wonder how that will work out for ya."

Selah put down one more of the training books she'd been studying. Pearl had grown tired of reading and had long since wandered off. Skunk whined and twitched as she slept at Grandpa's feet.

"There is lots to learn, and it's so fun."

"Horse training has come a long way since the Old West days. The cowboys would throw a rope to catch the horse. Then they'd snub the horse to a post and blindfold it. They'd toss a saddle on and cinch it up fast and tight. The cowboy would swing into the saddle, release the tie, pull the blindfold, and buck the horse out."

"I'd never let anybody do that to Dream."

"No, of course not. Now, trainers use a 'natural' approach. They study wild horses and how they interact with each other. From wild horses, we learn how to get a horse to respect us and be obedient to what is asked of it."

Selah admired her mare, standing out by the far pasture fence. "I'm going to go call her in again. It's so fun." Leaving Grandpa to his reading, she walked to the paddock. Anticipating her quick response, Selah called to Sweet Dream.

The mare turned her head and looked at Selah, but didn't move from the spot.

Selah called again, "Dream!"

The mare lowered and shook her head and neck. Her mane tossed from side to side.

"Dream!" Selah called a little louder.

This time the agitated mare reared. She balanced on her hind legs for several seconds, before dropping back to the ground. The mare refused to budge. Her nose flipped up and down in quick bursts.

"Something is wrong with Dream." Selah followed the fence out to where Dream stood rooted.

Her cat lay at the mare's feet. The beautiful cat stretched out on her side, motionless.

"Pearl!" Selah rushed to her, paused, and glared at Dream. "Dream, how could you? How could you hurt my Pearl?" She scooped up the cat, held her like a baby, and ran to the barn. Sweet Dream trotted next to the fence following Selah as far as the fence allowed her to go. "Get away, you evil thing. You've done enough damage."

"Grandpa!"

At the alarm in her voice, he looked up from his reading and rose from the chair. The cat hung limp in Selah's arms.

"Take her right to the truck, Selah."

Grabbing his keys off the hook, he met Selah at the truck in time to open the door. He helped her maneuver herself and her precious kitty inside. The truck roared to life, and they wasted no time.

"Grandpa, why would Dream do this to Pearl?"

"Hard to say. You can't forget she is wild."

"If Dream did this to Pearl... Then maybe you're right, Grandpa. Maybe she should go back to Miss Laura."

Grandpa looked quickly over at her and back to the road without comment.

Arriving shortly at the small animal clinic, they were ushered into a cold exam room with stainless steel cabinets. The rubbing alcohol assaulted and tingled her nose. The chill from the brilliant white lights dug bone deep. Selah tenderly laid Pearl on the metal exam table. The cat's breathing was so shallow and slight she couldn't tell if Pearl was even breathing. Looking anxiously at Grandpa, she hovered over Pearl as if she could add breath to the cat's still body. His concern deepened the crevasses of his face.

She pictured Dream standing over Pearl. *If you did this to Pearl, I'll never forgive you, Dream.*

The young vet pried open the cat's eyes and flicked a light across her pupils. He opened her mouth and shined his light down her throat. With his stethoscope, he listened to her heart and lungs. His fingers worked through every inch of her fur, searching for an answer to the mystery.

"She's been snakebit." The vet delivered the grim news. "See here on her leg." He pulled the hair back. "These puncture wounds are fang marks. The surrounding tissue is red and swollen."

Relief and alarm swamped Selah. "Dream didn't do it, Grandpa! Will my Pearl be all right, Dr. Robinson?"

"I can start her on fluids to help flush her system. I shouldn't give her anti-venom without knowing what kind of snake it was. The likelihood of an allergic response to anti-venom is high."

"I didn't see a snake. Oh, my Pearl!" She gasped through her tears.

"We will do everything we can for her, Selah. At least the bite is on an extremity and not on her body anywhere. It would help if we knew what kind of snake it was."

Selah's put her face next to Pearl and rested her fingers delicately on her shoulder.

"She will need to stay here. We have to keep her hydrated, warm, and quiet."

"I can't leave her!"

"There is nothing more we can do here, Selah," Grandpa said gently. "The best thing for Pearl is to let the doc do his job. Let's head home now."

Selah ran her hand ever so gently down the cat's fur and kissed her goodbye. "You...fight...back. You hear me, Pearl?"

Leaving the cat in Dr. Robinson's hands, the pair rode home in silence.

When they got to the farm, Sweet Dream still stood over the spot where Selah had found Pearl.

"That's strange. Don't you think it's strange, Grandpa?"

"Yes, it is odd. Her hay hasn't been touched. She does have plenty of grass, though, so she may not need the extra hay. Let's walk on out there and take a look around."

Sweet Dream stood as if cemented in place. As they approached, she snorted menacingly then lowered her head and flipped it up and down a couple times. She lightened in the front end and lifted her hooves from the ground. From a half rear, Dream struck out with one hoof and stomped the ground when she landed. She snorted again and repeated the process.

"She is bothered by something up there with her." Then Selah saw the snake. It was pulverized almost beyond recognition. "Dream hates snakes."

The mare continued to snort, rear, and strike at it.

"Looks that way, and she doesn't trust that it's dead," Grandpa said.

Skunk went along on the hunt, but when she spotted the dead intruder, she made a beeline out of the pasture. Skunk plopped down a safe distance away. "Good girl." Grandpa nodded. "A good farm dog knows not to mess with evil."

"And a great horse stomps on evil. Look, Grandpa. Sweet Dream has talent."

"I've never heard of a snake-killing horse. I hope she left enough of it for me to tell what it is."

He picked up a long stick and stirred the tattered snake around. "No bright colors, so it's not a coral snake. Wrong color and shape for a cottonmouth. I don't see any rattles. By default, that makes it a copperhead."

"Do you think it's the snake that bit Pearl?"

"I don't think it's just a nasty coincidence." He scooped up the more-than-dead snake on the stick and carried it to the barn, with Sweet Dream right behind him.

Selah and Skunk gave them plenty of space.

"Let's call Dr. Robinson and tell him what we found. Then I'll dispose of it so all the animals can settle down."

Selah crowded his elbow while he made the call. She leaned in to hear Dr. Robinson. "There is no change in Pearl. She is still unresponsive and in grave condition. I'm glad you think you identified the snake. I'll give her anti-venom for pit viper. We'll know more in the morning."

Selah left the house with a heavy heart. She blindly made her way to the stall. She knew she was to keep a fence between her and Sweet Dream, but her mind was preoccupied with the afternoon's drama and the threat hanging over Pearl's life. She hurried to the mare grazing out in the field.

The mare lifted her head as she approached. Dream tensed when Selah threw herself around her neck, but the mare stood stock still.

"I'm sorry I doubted you." Selah told Sweet Dream all about her princess cat. "Who else would care, except you, that Pearl wouldn't step in a puddle or touch a mouse? Who else would care that Pearl always sleeps on her own small pillow, in our princess-pink room? Who else would care that Pearl likes to walk on the piano keys?" Dream stood by Selah as she poured out her grief.

The flashlight beam found her in the pasture. Grandpa walked out to them. He put his arm around her shoulders and led her back to the house without saying a word.

"I'm sorry I didn't tell you where I was going. How did you know where to find me?"

"Easy," he said. "Looked for you in the same place I would look for your grandmother when the world crashed in on her. A horse listens to the words you say and hears your heart."

Selah headed up the stairs to her room. She stopped on the stairs and turned back to him. "I thought you would scold me for being in the pasture. Honest, I didn't even know where I was going until I got there."

He nodded. "Sweet Dream handled herself fine. Maybe she has learned a thing or two since she arrived."

Not the time to tell him Dream knocked me into the stall wall and then ripped my jeans. Besides, I'm sure she is sorry. Selah ran down the stairs and hugged Grandpa before heading up again to wait for the dark night to be over.

"God, I know you hear me. Please heal my kitty. I love her so much." With nothing else she could do, Selah slipped under the sheets. She lay for a long while listening to the silence in the house. A new peacefulness surrounded her, and without even realizing it, she dropped off to sleep.

When her eyes opened in the morning, Selah's first thought was *Pearl.* Breakfast was a quiet affair. It all looked good, but Selah just stirred her food around on the plate. "I need to touch her, Grandpa."

"Of course you do, sunshine." He kissed the top of her head.

Grandpa and Selah left the breakfast mess and headed to town. As he pulled off into the local donut shop, she grinned at him.

Donuts might help. She was grateful for the sense of peace still with her. She didn't know what would happen with Pearl, only that it was all out of her hands.

The clinic was still dark as they rolled up to the curb by the front door, but the doc's truck was parked on the side of the brick building. Walking around to the back door, Selah knocked tentatively. As they were about to turn to go back and wait in the truck, the door pushed open, and a disheveled but smiling Dr. Robinson greeted them. "I was just about to call you. Our kitty is awake this morning."

Selah hurried to the cage, easing open the door. Reaching in, she wanted to feel Pearl for a hint of a breath for herself. The cat was still quiet and weak, but she was breathing. Grateful, Selah turned to Dr. Robinson to thank him when she noticed the cot against the clinic wall, its blanket flipped half off onto the floor.

"Oh, Dr. Robinson, you're the greatest. You stayed here with my Pearl."

"No fuss needed, Selah. It's what I would've done for my own daughter's cat. I am heading home for a few hours to get some sleep and a shower before the clinic opens this morning. Pull the door shut when you leave, and it will lock itself."

"Don't know how to thank you, Doc," Grandpa said.

"Wait till you get my bill."

"Some folks earn their superhero capes by fighting fires. Some by staying up all night nursing a special cat," Grandpa told Selah.

Selah and Grandpa pulled chairs up by Pearl and plunged into the bag of donuts. "These are delicious, Grandpa."

"Do you know your pretty little face is dusted with white powder?"

"Well, you have strawberry jelly all over your chin." She crinkled her nose at him.

"Pearl is going to be fine. I know it." She stroked the cat with her finger and whispered encouragement to her. "Dream took care of that mean snake for you, Pearl. It didn't even look like a snake when she was done with it. That's what a friend does." Selah peered at Grandpa to see if he was listening before she shared her secret with Pearl. "I wish Dream would be that kind of a friend to me instead of ripping off my pockets."

CHAPTER THIRTEEN

As Grandpa led the mare to the round pen, Selah skipped behind them, causing the mare to prance and look back over her shoulder at the energy following her. Selah went over her mental notes from the training videos. She rehearsed her moves like she was getting ready to do a Broadway play. "Point, cluck, slap the ground. Step in front, back up, move the training stick to the other hand, and point in the opposite direction. I think I got it."

Then, there she was, face to face with a creature who didn't speak English. "I need to learn to speak horse." Immobilized for a moment, the two stood and sized each other up. Selah raised her arm and pointed her finger.

Dream's legs braced, and her hooves spread as if the horse was ready to go in any direction. Her dark eyes watched the intensity in the form of a small girl.

Selah clucked. Nothing happened. So she spanked the ground with the training stick the way she'd seen Cooper do it.

All Dream's legs exploded off the ground in an effort to get away from this great danger dressed in pink. She threw dirt and sand in a cloud that enveloped Selah.

Spitting out the grit, Selah said, "Maybe this is not going to be as easy as the video makes it seem."

The mare ran around the pen like a gerbil on a wheel. Her head ducked down between her knees, and she bucked like a pro. She moved too close to Selah on the circle and kicked toward her.

Grandpa yelled, "Point and swing the stick to hit the ground hard. Let her know she is in trouble for that."

The horse spun toward Selah, reared, and struck out. When her hooves hit the ground again, she stood tall and tense and blasted a snort. Defiance blew out her nostrils.

Grandpa commanded Selah. "Come out—*now!*"

"I can't quit now. Dream will think she won."

"She has won, and she is getting aggressive. She's not the horse for you."

Selah kept one eye on Dream. "I have to try again."

"It's not worth getting hurt. If this is what she is made of, then she is a bad match for you. I want you out of there."

"I can't give up."

He nodded, but moved to the gate of the pen, moving into position to intervene if it got any uglier.

"I can do this! Dream can do this!"

"Lord, help me—you're just like your grandma!"

"That's a good thing, right?" She lifted her arm to give direction.

The mare moved out as her head shook in displeasure, flipping her mane from one side to the other.

Selah slapped the ground with the training stick and made the mare canter and canter some more.

Grandpa called out moves. "Walk with her in your own smaller circle. Now, step over in front of her, ask her to come with your finger, and run backward. She's looking at you. Point. Point. Now drive her forward. That's a girl. Good job."

Selah squealed, "I get it. I get it. She did it. She understood I wanted her to go the other way. Wow. This is more fun than anything." After a dozen more turns, Selah began to understand the rhythm, and Dream started acting like she was tired.

"Watch for her to soften," he called. "She is keeping her ear on you. Look for one more sign. There it is. She's licking her lips. Stop. Ask her to come in with your finger and body language. If she comes… There ya go. Stand still, relax, and let her come to you. Keep her a safe distance from you, though. Now rub her with the training stick, right between her eyes. Turn away from her. Now walk away. She is following you, Selah. Keep walking. Stop, pet her face again with the stick, and leave. One more time. Now just stand there with her."

"It's like she's deciding if I am her leader or not?"

"That is exactly what she is doing. The problem is, Dream acts like she is queen and you are not. You had to work her really hard to get even a little sign of submission. That tells me a lot about how she's wired, and none of it's good. Now, come on out so I can rest."

"You weren't doing anything."

"Okay then, why do I feel like I just ran a hundred miles?" He sat heavily in his lawn chair and kicked his boots out in front of him. "She will test your leadership at every opportunity. Not turning to face you when you go into her stall. She'll try to go through a gate first. You have to catch those signs early."

"I'm okay with her going through the gate first."

"If subtle disrespect is allowed to take root and grow, the horse will become more aggressive with you. That's dangerous and not good for your health because you are not another nine-hundred-pound horse. If they don't respect you, they will hurt you."

She perched on a log while they watched the mare. Selah hung on every word from Grandpa. She wanted to learn everything—just everything. She couldn't wait to go again, but Grandpa said, "We need to tie her to the pole in the shade. She needs personal quiet time so she can process what she learned today."

"Looks like standing tied isn't her favorite thing," Selah said as the mare walked around the post flipping her nose.

Dream stopped, stretched her neck up high, and nickered out her displeasure to the world. After a pause, she resumed her marching and nose flipping.

"She is always flipping her nose. It's actually really cute, don't ya think, Grandpa?"

"There is nothing cute about a disrespectful, aggressive horse."

CHAPTER FOURTEEN

*G*randpa heaved himself up from his chair and put his hand
out to encourage Selah off her log.

"Can we call and check on Pearl?" she asked.

"Yes, then we need to call your mom and dad. You remember
they're coming down tomorrow, right?" His hand on her shoulder,
they walked to the house.

"I can't leave now. Not with just getting started with Dream.
Not with Pearl in the clinic."

"Selah, I need to rest. You're a lot to keep up with."

"You love it and you know it."

"Call your parents and ask if you might be able to stay a little
longer. Try nicely."

"Like forever?"

"Not forever."

"I could live here with you, Grandpa. I wouldn't be any
trouble."

"Hah. What makes you think you aren't any trouble? You live an hour away. I'll come and pick you up more often."

"It's not the same. You know it's not the same. My brothers drive me crazy anyway."

"That's what brothers do best. Your mom needs you to help with your little brothers. And your family wants time with you this summer. Aren't you all scheduled to go camping in a few weeks? It seems to me you were looking forward to going."

Selah puckered up her sad face. "Well, I was. *Before* Sweet Dream."

"What do you want in your smoothie?" Grandpa popped the lid off the blender.

"Yum… banana, orange juice, and please, no spinach."

"My dear, you can't even taste the spinach."

"Maybe not, but it turns it all yucky green."

"Nothin' wrong with green." As the blender stopped its racket, the phone rang. He poured her smoothie into a tall glass, popped in a straw, and slid it to her. "Hello… Doc. We were just going to call you." He looked at Selah sipping her drink and smiled the doctor's good news at her. "Great news, Doc. Thank you."

Grandpa leaned toward Selah and beamed her a smile "Dr. Robinson said Pearl is awake now and trying to sit up. She is still mostly sleeping, but he sees good progress. He said if she starts eating, he will take the IV out tomorrow afternoon and send her home."

"Great news makes even the spinach you snuck into my smoothie taste good. When we get Pearl home, I'm going to spoil her rotten."

"Too late. She's already rotten, just like somebody else I know." Raising his eyebrows at her, he dialed the phone. "Hey, Karen, it's Ed. Are you and Daniel still coming tomorrow?"

Selah bit down on her straw. *I can't leave now. They can't make me.*

"Great, we're looking forward to seeing everyone. Selah's here and wants to say hi." Grandpa passed the phone.

"Hi, Mom. Yes, I'm good, great actually. We had a couple scary days because a snake bit Pearl, but she is going to be all right. She can probably come home tomorrow. Sweet Dream is fantastic. We worked in the round pen for the first time. Grandpa said I did great. He was kinda chapped at Dream, though."

The boys buzzed in the background. One of them was pretending to be Super Something and the other Super Sidekick.

"Mom, can I stay with Grandpa a little longer?" Selah frowned. "But, Mom, Pearl's going to need extra love, and we just started with Sweet Dream."

"No, honey you'll be coming home with us. I need you here."

The frown deepened on her face. "Dream needs me too." Outside Dream walked around the post flipping her nose. "Grandpa can bring me home in time to go camping." She looked over at Grandpa, who nodded without looking up from the newspaper. "He says he will."

"That's because he doesn't know how to say no to you."

"I don't want to come home. I need to stay." Selah chewed on her straw.

"You watch your attitude, young lady. We love you. See you tomorrow."

"Yes, ma'am. Love ya back."

"She said no?" Grandpa asked.

"Pretty much. She wasn't going for it. I don't know how to convince her how important this is to me. She said to tell you she's bringing plenty of food for tomorrow, so not to worry about feeding them." Selah mangled her straw. "Can Sweet Dream be turned out now?"

"She's been tied an hour, and she needs longer than that. Double at least. Go check on her, though."

Selah picked up one of the training books, pulled a carrot from the fridge drawer, and hiked to be with Dream.

The mare's head and neck lifted, and both little pointed ears flicked forward as she watched Selah approach.

Selah dropped the book in the lawn chair. Dream practically inhaled the carrot bribe, and Selah rubbed the mare with both hands. When she reached her withers, she scratched with all her fingers. "That's your sweet spot," Selah cooed.

The mare extended her neck, twisted her head way over, and her lips flapped like a goldfish out of air.

"Ridiculous, you look like a goof."

Selah broke away and ran back to the house. "Grandpa, may I work on Sweet Dream's mane? She still looks like a wildebeest. She is letting me scratch her withers."

"Okay, if you're careful." He put down the mail. "I'll need to cross tie her though, so she can't kick you." With Dream secured by the tack room, Selah began trying to comb the knots from her thick, matted mane. "This is next to impossible, Dream. What a beautiful mess you are."

An hour later, she'd barely worked though half the mane. Determined, Selah kept detangling one knot at a time, starting from the ends and working to the root. It all went so well she relaxed handling Dream and forgot about Grandpa warning her to be careful. White teeth flashed a split second before she felt the belt loop on her jeans jerk away.

She leaped back. "What a bad girl! You have to stop doing that." She looked around to see where Grandpa was. "You're lucky Grandpa didn't see it! He'd be on the phone right now sending you away. Don't you want to stay? Keep your nasty teeth to yourself."

With renewed caution, Selah un-twirled the last few strands of mane. Finally, she stepped back to admire her hard work. "I think you need a touch of pink."

Selah ran to the house, burst through the door, and dashed up the stairs. Sitting cross-legged on the floor, she dumped the contents of her travel bag. "Cherry Bomb Pink. The perfect color for Dream." Grabbing a towel, some peroxide, and plastic bags, Selah headed outside when she had to pass Grandpa in the kitchen.

"Selah," he said sternly, "what are you up to? What are you doing with that stuff?"

"She needs some pink."

"Oh. Of course, she does." Grandpa rolled his eyes and looked to the heavens.

Selah scooted out the door and hurried to the mare, but stopped dead in her tracks. The mare was looking at her with big, wild, scared eyes. "Oh, it's just a towel. Maybe I shouldn't run at you with a big towel flapping. You might pull the whole barn down trying to escape. Someday, after I train you, not now." Selah backed up a little, and the mare dropped her head again. Selah flapped the towel, and when the mare looked in her direction, Selah stopped and backed up a step. "Ah... There ya go. Are you starting to realize this flapping beast isn't going to eat you?" She extended the towel so Dream could sniff it.

"Let the beauty makeover begin." She tucked the towel around Dream's neck, securing it with binder clips. Standing on a step stool far out in front and to the side of the mare, Selah examined the horse's dull white stripe down her face. "Ugh, it's too dirty just to color it. I'll bet Grandma had whitening shampoo for our paint horse somewhere." She remembered some bottles behind the door of the tack room. "Yes!" Selah eased the deep blue colored shampoo onto Dream's soon-to-be highlighted stripe with the greatest of care. It was too soon and too risky to attempt to shampoo the horse's dirty white hind sock. She separated a few strands of mane and dipped them in peroxide. Sliding the peroxided sections into the small plastic bags, she tied them off. She was careful not to splash the black mare with the shampoo or the peroxide. "Let's not do polka dots today." The whitening shampoo needed to stay on for a long while. She hadn't considered how she was going to rinse it out. She didn't know if Sweet Dream ever had a water bath. "Hummm. Getting the shampoo off your face might be a trick."

Dashing back to Grandpa, Selah asked, "Can you move her to the wash rack, please?"

He turned and tilted his head down, looking at her over the rim of his reading glasses. "Well, this could get exciting fast. I guess today is as good as any to teach her to take a bath. You couldn't have just tied some pink ribbon in her hair?"

"Oh, Grandpa, she will be beautiful."

Selah stood back as he added water to Sweet Dream's equation. He held the rope in one hand and the hose in the other. Starting at her feet, he worked up and down her legs before moving to her shoulder, gauging her reaction. Dream side-passed briskly in a circle around him. He kept her head tipped toward him and let the water flow down her leg. "Sweet Dream has met water before, since she's not too terrible." In an instant, the mare pulled back on the halter and scrambled backward. "Ah, a quiet moment with her is only the eye of the hurricane. Let's get to the worst of it. Are you ready for the whitener to be washed off her face?"

"Yes, I think it's been on long enough."

Grandpa turned the water nozzle to spray a heavy mist. The mare was prissy about even that much water on her face. Flipping her nose and stomping her foot, Dream made it clear the water in her face wasn't working for her. The mare's head and neck bobbed up and down, and she shook off the water furiously. He ignored her evasive antics and misted her face until he finished the job. "There is some regular shampoo-conditioner in the tack room if you want to finish it up right."

Before the whole sentence was even out of his mouth, Selah streaked back to the tack room and created a ruckus behind the door. She globbed shampoo into her hand and worked it into the mane. After pouring some onto a brush with rubber fingers, she scrubbed it into Dream's black coat. "She likes it Grandpa. Look at her face."

To Dream she whispered, "You watch how you behave because Grandpa is watching you." Staying well to the side, Selah reached around and pulled Dream's tail out to the side so she could work in some shampoo. "This is useless. These tail knots are massive."

"I could cut them out," he volunteered.

"You wouldn't!" Selah threw him her most shocked look. After a moment she sighed, "Isn't this the most delightful way to spend a day, Grandpa?"

"If you say so." He turned the water back on and rinsed the suds off.

Foamy soap floated down the horse's shoulder and legs. "She is so pretty, Grandpa. Just like I always dreamed my horse would look."

By the time he finished with the rinse, Sweet Dream's face was already dry. Selah pulled her stool back to the front of the mare and stepped up with Cherry Bomb Pink in hand. She dabbed a little color at the top of Dream's white stripe, up where the forelock would cover it in case it didn't come out just right. Leaning back to consider the look, she asked Grandpa, "What do you think?"

"I can't watch." He shook his head as he retreated to the house.

"Don't let him bother you, Sweet Dream. I think you look adorable." Selah blotted pink down the rest of her stripe. She dipped the bleached tips of her mane into the dye and held each one in the color to get them the brightest pink she could.

As Grandpa climbed the stairs to the porch, he tilted his head and peered underneath at Skunk, who peered back at him. "You've not come out from under there all afternoon have you?"

"She thinks I don't know she is hiding from me," Selah called. "No bath for you today, Skunk."

"You're one wise dog. If it had occurred to Selah earlier, you'd be sporting a pink highlight too."

Selah and her mare hung out together in the barn for the better part of the afternoon. "Dream, you are delightfully Cherry Bomb Pink. Just wait till Mom sees you. She has to understand that I have to be here with you. I'm not leaving you—end of story!"

CHAPTER FIFTEEN

Hearing the phone ring in the house, Selah scurried to pick it up, expecting a status report on Pearl. "Hello." Instead of the vet, a strange man said, "Hello. Is Ed there?"

Selah paused. Something about that voice? *I know that voice.* "Tell him it's Cooper."

Selah dropped the phone and ran outside screeching. "Grandpa! Grandpa! It's Mr. Cooper!"

Grandpa picked the phone up off the floor. "Hey there, friend. It's been awhile."

Selah leaned in so she could hear, but Grandpa shooed her away.

The conversation didn't take long. When he hung up, he wandered outside like nothing big happened. "Grandpa, that was Mr. Cooper! Aren't you going to tell me what he said?"

"He was just catching up on old times."

Selah gave him her best evil-eye imitation.

"All right, all right. Come sit with me. Actually, he called about you."

"Me? How would he know about me?"

"The article in the *Canaan Item*, that's how."

"For real? It is only my first name in the article."

"Well, yes, except I was in the picture. Remember? One of Cooper's trainers saw the article and put it on his desk. She thought it was a human-interest story he might enjoy. She didn't know we are old friends."

"Oh, I see." Her shoulders slumped with disappointment.

"No, I don't think you do. He loves the story of you and Sweet Dream, and he wants to meet you both. He's driving up out of Houston tomorrow after he finishes up a clinic and is going to stop by here."

"Oh wow, super great."

"Oh, it gets better."

"What? What? Tell me? Grandpa—talk faster!"

"Turning into a nice evening, isn't it? Think we might get some rain?"

"Tell me, pretty please, with sugar on top."

"Cooper wants to do a TV episode on you and Sweet Dream."

The high-pitched shriek escaping from her soul wasn't even recognizable as her own voice.

Poor Skunk dove under the porch.

Dream's head popped up out in the pasture. She stood looking at the house, watching for the creature that must be impaled on a stake for it to make such an unearthly racket.

Selah jumped up and down, bringing her knees all the way to her chest. Alternating between squealing and screeching, she blasted off the porch into the grass. There her leaping and dancing continued with great abandon.

Sweet Dream was putting on a show of her own out in the pasture. The mare moved toward the house in a cadenced prance, and then wheeled in a complete circle.

Grandpa rose to his feet to watch the commotion. "The mare looks the very image of her mother."

Selah felt like an explosion of joy. Puffing from exertion, she stopped and followed his fixed gaze to Sweet Dream. She slowly absorbed that the mare was doing dressage, on her own, out in the pasture.

Grandpa muttered dressage movements, "Piaffe, perfect volte, canter pirouette, piaffe. Extraordinary, quite extraordinary."

Selah could see the very moment when the mare decided the excitement must be over and she'd lost enough weight exerting herself. Dream froze, looking toward Selah, and then dropped her head to graze—her best talent.

After a few moments, Selah broke the hush with a quiet, appreciative, "Awesome".

"Harmony is certainly her mother," he said. Grandpa held his cap in his hands and fidgeted with the brim. "I have a confession to make." He slapped his hat back on his head. "Your grandmother had Illusion bred when she retired the mare from the show circuit. Long story short. Harmony is a great-great-granddaughter of Illusion."

"So Dream is Illusion's bloodline? That explains everything! You look at Harmony and then look at Dream and you think Dream was adopted. That means Dream will be able to do the reining spin and stop."

"Yes, it likely does. Harmony is the result of a cross with a Warmblood stallion because your grandma was looking for a dressage mount. Illusion came from champion Morgan Horse bloodlines.

Dream's father is Presidential Bid, the greatest Morgan reining horse of all time." Grandpa bit his upper lip. "What I didn't know was, after you were born, your grandma told Laura that when you became eight, the next foal she raised would be for you. That's why Laura couldn't give up trying to find Dream. She is your grandma's dream for you."

Selah turned to look at Grandpa with astonishment on her face. "I knew it! I knew deep in my heart that Dream was sent from heaven. She is incredible, and God and Grandma gave her to me."

Sleeping was just out of the question. Tomorrow could be the biggest day or the worst day of her whole life. Pearl was healed and coming home. "This bed feels empty without Pearl. And, pinch me, Mr. Cooper is coming to meet me and Dream."

Why can't I stay here? Mom is so stubborn. If my parents insist I go home, it will ruin everything.

CHAPTER SIXTEEN

*R*emembering the terrifying trailer ride always causes my heart to race. I don't know what happened, but skidding down the road sideways is not the way horses are supposed to travel. It got so bumpy I had to scramble to stay up on my feet. Then the trailer jerked to a stop. My hind legs slipped out from under me as the impact slammed me to the floor. I was scared and frantic to get out. I thrashed and struggled. I had to get loose of the tie and free of the partition. But the metal can they made me ride in wouldn't let me go.

Then lights and sirens flew toward me. Rearing, I kept hitting my head on the roof. I couldn't control my panic or think straight. I threw myself side to side, desperate to get free. Nothing worked. I was stuck and terrified.

The man who loaded me didn't come to help me. A strange man opened the door, and I didn't trust him. When the partition released me, I threw myself backward with every ounce of strength I had left. I jerked on the rope. When it broke away, I plunged out of the trailer.

Mangled metal ripped gashes in my sides. My feet couldn't grip the slick road. I fell so hard the breath crushed out of me. The gravel road tore skin from my legs, and little rocks embedded in my flesh.

The man in the uniform tried to grab the remnant of lead rope hanging from my halter as I struggled to my feet. Nothing, let alone a mere man, was going to hold me now. My hooves pounded the ground. My heart pounded the same rhythm as my hooves. People in cars stared at me with their mouths hanging open as I powered past them all. Had they never seen a horse before?

Stark terror gave me the determination and strength to run for my life. Never, ever would I consider getting back into one of those metal monsters. They can't be trusted.

A break in the trees on the roadside revealed a grassy path, and I veered onto it. I galloped until I was sure I was safe from the lights and sirens—and the trailer.

I slowed my pace to a canter and then a dogtrot. I needed water. I trotted on without seeing anything I recognized. And not one water trough anywhere. No horse barns full of fresh hay and stall shavings like I'd had all my life.

I moved through the fields of grass. Surely, I'd find other horses out here somewhere—a herd of friendly, nice mares that would help me. They could show me where the water was.

I paused in the shade of a cluster of tall pines and oaks at the edge of the grass clearing. With the sun going down, I realized I was alone in a forest full of things that wanted to eat me. My pasture and stall at home were safe. My mother and the other mares at the farm all looked out for me. We stuck together through the scary things. Like the time the bobcat skirted the edge of our pasture. My mother told me it was best to stay away from all predators. I was easy to convince after the bobcat let out a hair-raising scream.

I bet the other horses my age are glad I'm lost. My dam was the boss mare so the other foals were jealous of me. But that wasn't the biggest reason they didn't like me.

The lady, who took care of us, treated me special. She liked me best, and all the other horses knew it. She brought me extra food and scratched me on my favorite spot on my withers. She was always telling me about another lady who dreamed of me. It didn't make any sense to me. But she would cry, and I'd try to cheer her up by breathing on her neck. She smelled like peppermint. I know she's looking for me.

As it got dark, I skittered and startled at every sound. I never used to be afraid of the dark, but then I'd never stayed out at night by myself before. I tried to lie down to sleep, but lying on my folded legs hurt. Instead, I locked my knees and slept on my feet. I needed to be ready to escape anyway. Blood dripped down my legs as I slept.

The next day found me weary, thirsty, and afraid. As I walked along a well-worn trail, I smelled something important—a crisp and clear scent. Following my nose, I found a small, fresh spring tucked into a stand of brush and trees. The grass around it grew thick and in clumps. I walked into the cool water and dropped my head like it was a boulder. Water had never tasted so good. After filling my tummy, I stood, letting the water wash the wounds on my legs. I snatched the delicious water grass. I dropped to my knees and sank into the healing waters, flushing my wounds. It refreshed me. I rested in the coolness and looked around at my new reality. My new life on my own.

From then on, life just went by day after day. Then one night, the clouds covered the moon, blotting out any light. What happened next was that crazy old owl's fault. I had told him before to stay away from me. As he swooped down and nabbed that nasty snake, he dangled it right under my nose as he flew off. Well, I can tell you it startled me. When I leaped to the side of the trail, I planted both my front feet into a wad of old wire. Who knew where it came from?

The wire wouldn't let me go. If I struggled, I knew I would lose the battle. As luck would have it, none of the coyote pack had passed me in the night. When I could see better, I thought I'd be able to pull my feet out. It didn't work out though. I was totally helpless.

It didn't take long for the buzzards to find me the next morning. They smelled my blood. They weren't taking any chances getting too close, just yet. They knew I still had my teeth to defend myself. I would fight them with every breath. The buzzards were patient and stood around in clusters, mocking me. They would crowd up to me and look me right in the eye. They would wait to pounce when my strength failed.

Then a small girl and a dog that looked like a skunk came hurrying toward me. I was frightened to see a person after so long, especially one running at me. I couldn't get up and I couldn't get away so what choice did I have anyway? If they were going to eat me, I hoped they would make it quick.

Look how it turned out. I am in a safe paddock guarded by a skunk. A prissy cat pal seems to like me too. And the most intriguing of all is my new little friend whose hand sometimes has a carrot in it. She is very brave. Those buzzards would have eaten me except for her and the skunk. It wasn't nice of me to try to scare her in the round pen, but I needed to know if I could trust her not to hurt me if I did something she didn't like.

Wonder what the mares at home would think if they could see me now with my new touch of pink. Life is going to be good here, and I can get used to pink.

The mare turned when the front door to the house squeaked open. In the darkness, Selah made her way to Dream. The little horse nickered and walked to greet her.

"Can't you sleep either, Sweet Dream? And you have no idea what is about to happen tomorrow. I have to go home. I will miss you so much. I think you might miss me too. Mr. Cooper will love you. Grandpa said he wants us to do a training video for his TV show. That's just super cool. We could be on our way to Hollywood. Somehow, we have to convince Mom that we need to be together."

Selah's arms slipped naturally around her mare's neck. Her fingers laced and locked together just like their two hearts. "My Sweet Dream. They can never take me from you. I won't let it happen."

CHAPTER SEVENTEEN

Selah's Uncle Christopher and cousin, Anderson, arrived first. Grandpa went to meet them and high-fived with Anderson while Christopher downloaded the junk from his car into a pile on the ground. Locating his laptop, he commandeered a table and arranged his workstation on the deck. Meanwhile, Anderson dragged the old box of cars and trucks to the sand pile to set up for some serious road excavation. Selah thought he might be getting a little old for making roads in the sand, or he might grow up to be an engineer. When he finished in the sand pile, it always looked like an elaborate city on a hill. She and Anderson were the same ages, barely a month apart. Selah watched him from the upstairs window. He looked just like Uncle Christopher with his dark hair and animated dark eyes. He liked horses almost as much as she did, but maybe, he liked trucks a little more. Anderson's favorite book was *The Black Stallion*. She liked that about him because it was her favorite book too.

The SUV honked in the yard. It barely stopped in front of the house when the doors flipped open. Her little brothers, both dressed in their red superhero shirts, launched out as if they were expelled from a cannon. It was like a trumpet heralded that the festivities should begin.

Skunk added to the merriment with her own rendition of "the gang's all here". Her barking and howling gave voice to the chaos. She leapt in the air and on the boys until they were all rolling around in the grass together. Skunk broke away and ran at top speed in a circle around them. Sprinting up and over the sand pile, she sprayed sand all over Anderson, disturbing his road maze.

"Hello, boys," Grandpa called. "Looks like Skunk's happy to see you."

The boys ran and wrapped themselves around his legs. They chattered away, not bothering to take turns.

Grandpa ruffled up their red hair. "Michael, you are built like a little fire plug, and your hair gets redder every year. How old are you going to be next week?"

"Five."

"Davy, what happened to your two front teeth?"

"They are under my pillow. I'm still hoping there's a tooth fairy."

"It doesn't keep you from putting on a smile the size of Texas. Hey, Anderson's already in the sand pile." Grandpa pointed the way to the fun.

Selah flew down the steps, into her mom's arms, and wrapped herself around her thin frame. Mom smelled of lavender and honey. Her dad came around and bear-hugged the two of them.

"Hello, Karen, Daniel," Grandpa said.

"Hi, Dad. Selah got the best of you yet?" Dad pulled away and winked at her.

Impatient already with all the pleasantries, Selah wanted to introduce the newest, greatest thing that ever happened in the family. "Come and meet Sweet Dream," she interrupted, twining her fingers with Mom and drawing everyone toward the paddock.

"Oh my goodness. Look at her," Mom said. "She's so pretty with her pink stripe. And it's remarkable how she looks like a mini-Harmony."

Her dad dutifully looked, but said, "Yup. Looks like a horse to me." He walked away to visit with Grandpa.

"She was doing dressage movements in the pasture all by herself last night," Selah bragged.

"Can we ride her?" Davy asked.

"No way, silly. She has to be trained first."

Since the horse wasn't going to be a ride, the brothers wandered off with Skunk in search of adventure.

Anderson, on the other hand, hung by the fence and watched the horse. "Wow. You're lucky, Selah. I've been asking Grandpa if we could get a horse, but he always said 'I don't think so'."

"Did your dad tell you her mom is Grandma Mary's horse?"

"Yeah."

"It's almost like God led her home. It's not like I went shopping for a horse, Anderson. She came to me, and now she's mine."

"I get the idea, Selah." Anderson made a face at her and resumed his road excavation.

"She is beautiful, Selah." Mom rubbed her shoulder. "I can see why you're taken with her."

"Yes, I love her so much, and she's only been here a few days." Selah scuffed the toe of her boot in the dirt, wanting to explain to Mom in just the right way. "I've already started her in the round pen, and I think she is doing great. Grandpa thinks she's too wild.

That's why it's so important that I stay here with her. I have to keep working with her every day so she'll learn to trust me."

"Horses are not more important than family. I thought we covered this last night. You've been here long enough, and it's time for you to come home."

Selah stood tall and looked her mother right in the eye. "You don't understand! I have to be here now! I need to work her every day."

"You're coming home, Selah, and that is final."

"You're just mean! You never let me do what I want."

"Selah! Do not talk to me like that. One more word with that tone, and you will be grounded for two weeks. You think about that, young lady."

Anger burned Selah's eyes, and her jaw locked. But she said, "Yes, ma'am." *This is not fair—not fair! Mom so doesn't understand me.* She chewed on the inside of her mouth. *If I make Mom any madder, this will turn ugly. I will lose for sure.*

Her mom looked hard at her for a long minute then turned without another word and went to the deck. Grandpa and Dad stretched out in the big wicker rockers watching Christopher. His tall, thin frame slumped over his laptop reading term papers. Dad had the same solid shape as Grandpa and the same full head of hair. Dad's hair was still mostly brown, though.

"You got more than you bargained for keeping Selah this time," Dad said.

"Yes, I sure did. It's been great having her here, though. Anything could happen with her around," Grandpa said.

"Don't talk about me like I'm not here," Selah snipped, still a little edgy after her talk with Mom.

"I hope you don't mind, Karen. We're about to have some

company arrive for lunch," Grandpa said. "I didn't know they were coming when I talked to you yesterday."

"Oh. Glad I made plenty. Who's coming?"

Grandpa looked at Selah, and she put her finger to her mouth to shush him. "I'm not at liberty to say just yet."

"You two are full of mystery and intrigue today," Dad said. "You and Selah look like you have swallowed canaries."

"The mystery will be revealed at the proper time. I can't take away her surprise."

As the men good-naturedly argued about which team might go to the World Series, Mom and Selah transferred the food from the SUV into the kitchen without speaking. Selah dodged the brothers as they streaked by the house. Davy's seven-year-old feet were leading the charge. Mike kept up as best he could. All the little noisemakers churned by on their way from one great adventure to another. Selah wasn't sure if Skunk was in hot pursuit or if she was trying to herd the boys together. Anderson concentrated on his engineering project until the brothers toppled him over in the sand. They grunted boy noises as they rolled around and wrestled.

Once Selah started on her story about finding Sweet Dream, she talked like an animated windup doll stuck in high gear. The story poured out like a gush of hot wind as she mesmerized her family with her retelling of the story of saving Sweet Dream from the buzzards. Her gaze darted down the driveway every few minutes, watching for her visitor to arrive and change everything—including Mom's mind.

CHAPTER EIGHTEEN

The boys blasted up on the deck. "A huge truck's comin'."

The family moved to the edge of the deck as the van eased down the driveway. The road had just enough bend to challenge the oversized horse transport. A scene of horses running through tall grasses was painted on the large, box van's sides. It eased to a stop, and the motor coughed and stilled. The family continued to stare. Grandpa looked over and winked at Selah.

She leaned to him. "My heart's beating so hard—it seems like everybody should be able to hear it."

A tall, thin man in boots, jeans, and a starched shirt climbed down from a side door of the van. The van driver and a slight young woman trailed him. The man marched confidently up to the deck with his hand out to Grandpa. They grasped hands and patted each other on the back.

"It's good to see you, Ed. I'm sorry I haven't been in touch. It's been too long."

"Cooper, you're a sight for sore eyes. Quite a rig you travel in these days."

"Well, friend, you gotta look the part, ya know. Say, is this your granddaughter I've heard so much about?"

"Yes. Cooper, I'd like you to meet, Selah. Selah, this is Mr. Cooper."

"I've heard a lot of girl-meets-horse stories. Never one quite like yours." Cooper smiled at her.

"Yes, sir. I can hardly believe it either."

Grandpa introduced his friend, who introduced his staff, to the rest of the family. "Cooper, do you want to unload Mariah? I have a pasture she can make use of while we have lunch."

"She would love that. She's been working pretty hard without a break." Cooper motioned to Miss Jordan, his assistant, to get his mare out.

Selah was right on Jordan's heels. To Selah, the jet-black mare inside was a rock star. Awe kept her hushed as Miss Jordan unloaded the famous mare and released her in Grandpa's pasture. Grazing was serious horse business. The mare dropped her head and snatched all the grass she could stuff in before she had to stop and chew.

Selah laughed at Mariah. "She looks like a little kid in a field full of Easter candy."

"She does look happy to mow your pasture."

"Do you get to ride Mariah, Miss Jordan?" Selah asked, never taking her eyes off the celebrity mare.

"No, Cooper rides her. Mariah is a one-man horse."

"How long have you been riding? How long have you been riding for Mr. Cooper?"

"I started riding about your age." Jordan brushed hay off

her jeans. Tightening up her ponytail, she explained, "I've been training for Cooper three-plus years."

"I saw you in one of Grandpa's colt starting videos. You sat in the saddle, but Mr. Cooper was telling the horse what to do."

"For a horse's first ride, that's a favorite training technique of Cooper's. It helps—"

Sweet Dream belted out a nicker to the visiting dignitary, overwhelming whatever else Jordan was about to say. Mariah ignored Dream's overture and snipped off every blade of grass under her nose before she inched forward.

In the meantime, Grandpa ushered everyone into the kitchen. Mom had laid out a huge bounty of food. They piled up their plates and moved out to the long table on the deck. Dad and Christopher filled plates for the boys and rang the triangle to call them. The boys gravitated to seats near George, the driver, and pestered him for stories about road trips.

Anderson asked, "How many states have you been to?"

Before George could answer, Davy asked, "Have you had any wrecks?"

Michael wanted to know, "Do you get to sleep in the truck?"

George answered the endless stream of questions like each one was the most important thing he'd ever been asked. He laughed louder at his stories than the boys did.

When Selah brought her plate to the table, she squeezed into an empty spot across from Mr. Cooper and next to her mom. She tilted her head and nodded along as Mr. Cooper talked about the clinic he'd just done.

"One lady brought me a horse that kept knocking her down. He wasn't so tough after all and was an easy fix." Cooper paused only long enough to chase his baked beans down with some sweet tea.

"The next horse took a little longer. The gelding would lie down under saddle and refuse to get up."

Grandpa leaned forward, propping his elbows on the table. "I remember a training clinic in Dallas when a horse Cooper was working in a round pen hit the top of the gate with its head. When the gate popped open, that horse took off for Houston. It left Cooper in the pen with his mouth hanging open. What a riot. I'm sure I'd never seen him speechless before."

"Glad you enjoyed it." Cooper smirked. "I remember when your grandpa was doing a demo in Conroe. A little lady brought him a Rocky Mountain mare to train. The lady just didn't bother to tell him the mare had a foal at home. They decided that very day to wean the baby rather than have to bring it along to the demo. That mare made so much racket looking for her foal that nobody could hear a word he said. Say, Ed? Did ya get her issues fixed? I couldn't hang around. It would have been unprofessional of me to stay since I was laughing so hard I could hardly stand up."

While Selah enjoyed the stories, she was starting to wonder if Mr. Cooper had forgotten about Sweet Dream. Her mom got up and removed the plates. When Selah started to get up to help, her mom put her hand on Selah's shoulder. "You stay and listen," she whispered.

In just a few minutes, Mom came back carrying a double layer chocolate cake. "You made my favorite. Thanks, Mom. This icing is so yum; I want a bowl of it to eat with a spoon."

With coffee and cake in front of him, Mr. Cooper's eyes shifted to Selah. "Pretty remarkable story you have to tell, young lady. Who could have ever seen that comin'? A filly out of your grandmother's mare stays hidden in the wilds behind your family farm."

"She is a miracle."

"Agreed. My viewers would love this story. I've been thinking about something since I first read the article on you.... I'd like for you and your family to consider..."

Selah reminded herself to breathe.

Turning to her parents, he said, "Would you consider allowing Selah and Sweet Dream to come to my ranch for about six weeks? I'd like to start Sweet Dream's training with my system. I could do a special on what happened and how they met. Selah would stay with Jordan, and she would learn right along with Sweet Dream."

Mom closed her eyes. Selah could tell that no was hanging on her Mother's lips. "That's the rest of the summer," Mom said. "I think she is way too young."

Selah's heart collapsed. Tears filled her eyes. She looked at her dad, whose face was noncommittal. Her eyes pleaded with Grandpa. *Please say something. What is wrong with you people? Can't you see how awesome cool this is?*

"Karen, would you feel better if I stayed with Selah?" asked Grandpa. "I could bring her home every weekend."

"Six weeks is a long time, Ed." Mom frowned. "I know you have responsibilities too. Anyway, can't you train the mare?"

"I could. It would take me a lot longer because I don't have the stamina I once did and I don't have Jordan. Because it would take me so much longer, there would inevitably be gaps in Selah's understanding of the technique."

Mom twisted slightly on the bench and leaned toward Grandpa "Well, so what if it takes longer? Selah's only twelve."

"I always thought you would teach Selah," Dad said.

"I think she would get more out of it if she did it with you." Mom crossed her arms and straightened up.

Selah ceased to enjoy her cake.

Grandpa smiled at Selah. "I'd get more out of it too, but the main issue concerning me is the wildness factor I see in the mare. Nobody is better with wild horses than Cooper. I know it's a tough decision, but it's an unbeatable offer. I think you might seriously consider it."

Mom looked out over the fields, and her expression stiffened.

Selah fought to keep the tears from welling up and over. Her wide eyes begged her mother.

"Daniel, can we walk?" Mom asked.

"Sure." Dad slipped his arm over her shoulder as they turned away.

Selah gnawed her inner cheek as her parents strolled down the path toward the Grasslands. Her heart was pleading, *Please, God.*

When Selah walked out to the pasture, Sweet Dream and Mariah were standing nose to tail with the fence in-between them. Both black mares were sleeping. Mariah's head bobbed a little in her sleep. Sweet Dream's tail swished every so often. It reminded the fly that had the nerve to land on her to keep moving. Selah admired the two mares from a distance so she didn't disturb their blissful sleep.

She could hear Grandpa and Mr. Cooper on the deck laughing. *God, will you make a way for us? I want to know everything they know about horses. I want to ride Dream like my grandma rode Illusion.* God's peace settled over her, and she smiled sweet gratitude.

Selah walked back to the house and sat on the bench next

to Grandpa. He put his arm around her and scooted her closer to him. The conversations around her droned on, and she was oblivious. Her leg jiggled like she had a twitch. "Grandpa?" she interrupted. "Has the vet called about Pearl?"

"No, not yet. Go on in and call 'em."

Selah nodded and moved off. She could hear her parents now, talking as they walked through the woods coming back toward the house. "Oooh. That didn't take long. That's a bad sign."

As the phone rang at the clinic, Selah watched her parents approach on the trail. She couldn't tell what they were thinking or might have decided. They looked so serious. *This can't be good.* Dr. Robinson answered the phone. "Dr. Robinson, this is Selah. I'm calling to see about Pearl."

"Pearl is recovering beautifully. I pulled her IV fluids, and she is eating and drinking just fine. She will need to stay on antibiotics for a few more days, but she is ready to go home whenever you can come get her."

"Oh, thank you so much, Dr. Robinson. I'll tell Grandpa. We have company at the farm right now, but we will come as soon as we can."

Selah bounced back out to the deck and shared the report on Pearl. Her parents sat quietly and looked a little grim. She searched their faces for a sign or a hint of a smile. Nothing. The boys bounded up on the deck with a dripping wet Skunk right behind them.

Selah's dad redirected them. "Boys, we passed a box turtle out on the trail."

Davy yelled, "Squirrel!" Their battle cry borrowed from an old movie. The brothers turned tail and raced for the forest trail. A soggy Skunk loped behind them.

The deck got quiet. Too quiet.

Mr. Cooper rose from the bench, nodded at them, and wandered over to talk to his assistants, giving the family some privacy.

"Well, Daniel?" asked Grandpa.

"Karen and I have prayed about this and talked about it, and we are in agreement that Selah can't go away by herself for six weeks. She is too young, and we don't know anything about the situation at the center."

Grandpa looked over at Selah. He already cradled one of her small hands in his own, and he began to rub it tenderly.

At least Grandpa's on my side. Selah sat in a stupor. She stared at her parents with no emotion in her eyes or on her face. Then she stood up and pulled her shoulders back. "You don't care about me or what I want. I'm no baby. I could take care of myself at the center."

"Before you melt down, Selah, hear us out," Dad said. "Your mom and I have serious misgivings about this idea and are reluctant to have you chasing after horse dreams. But we know this is terribly important to you. We understand what a great opportunity this is for you and Dream. So if Grandpa is willing to stay with you and bring you home to us every weekend, then we will allow it."

Selah lunged at her mom and nearly toppled her off the bench. "Thank you, Mom!"

"We're also going to look for a camping place closer to Mr. Cooper's ranch, so we'll still get some family time," Dad added.

"Thank you, Dad!" She burrowed in, hugging him. "This means so much to me."

"Guess you should go tell Mr. Cooper you'd like to accept his invitation," Grandpa suggested.

Selah didn't need to be told twice. She leaped from the deck, then struggled to walk calmly so she wouldn't appear childish to Mr. Cooper. The effort didn't work out too well when her joy overflowed and propelled her like a gazelle in full flight.

Grandpa chuckled, swirled the ice in his glass of tea, and drained the last of it.

As Selah raced away, tears sprang to her mom's eyes. "I knew this meant a lot to Selah, but I had no idea it went this deep."

"Hmmm," her dad mused. "Somewhere, her grandma must be smiling through her tears too."

"Indeed, yes." Grandpa grinned. "Horses are part of Selah's genetic code, and that, right there, is a picture of pure joy." He leaned closer to Selah's dad and added, "I'm not going to spoil Selah's moment, but that horse has got a wild streak a mile wide. I admit it worries me, and I'm glad Cooper's taking her on."

CHAPTER NINETEEN

Selah skipped back to the deck and squeezed into the rocker next to Grandpa as he outlined the family plan. "Sweet Dream will ride to the training facility with Mariah. Skunk will go home with my favorite little 'bedlam brothers'. I will drive Selah to the training center after making arrangements for Pearl. On Friday, I will drop Selah at home, pick up Skunk, and head to my farm."

"It'll be crazy, but so fun." Selah rubbed her hands together.

"On Sunday evening, we'll do it all in reverse," Grandpa finished.

Miss Jordan headed to the pasture to get Mariah and load the horse for her trip home. George was busy under the hood of the van, doing whatever. Selah watched Mr. Cooper pace the yard, deep in conversation on the phone, with one arm tight across his chest.

"We need to get Dream." Selah tugged on Grandpa's sleeve drawing him out of the chair.

Grandpa slung Dream's halter over his shoulder and headed to the paddock. Selah grabbed some carrots from the refrigerator and skipped to catch up with Grandpa. Dream followed Mariah until the fence stopped her.

"Look at her energy, Grandpa. She likes having a horse friend after so long." Selah sang out to her, "Dream!" Her head turned to look at Selah, and she hesitated only a moment before moving briskly toward her.

"Visions of carrots must be dancing in Dream's head," Grandpa said.

As the mare drew near, Selah extended the carrot and said, "I wouldn't disappoint you." Once haltered, Selah brushed her down. "You're riding with royalty, Dream. You be a lady. This is our shot. We're on our way. We're going to be amazing together. Everyone will see how wonderful you are."

Grandpa dug around in the tack room until he came up with an old pair of protective shipping boots that once belonged to Dream's mother. "They'll be a little tall on Dream, but better than nothing."

"Look everyone," Selah said. "Look at Dream." Dream was lifting her knees as high as she possibly could. "Dream, you're so funny."

The boys mimicked the horse walking and laughed till they complained their sides hurt.

"The boots feel odd to her, and she's not at all convinced she can walk in them," Grandpa said. Dream pranced on the end of the lead rope, exaggerating the action of her legs. "She's trying to figure the boots out. She'll get the hang of it soon."

"Ed, I meant to ask you, ah… what's with the pink?" Cooper chuckled.

"It'll grow on ya, but you better watch out, or Selah might convince Jordan that Mariah could use a little pink."

Grimacing, Cooper asked, "Has the mare been in a trailer since she got here?"

"No, Dr. Steve came out here. I've been wondering how she will load considering what Laura told me about the accident. It'll be interesting to see how she reacts to the van."

Hands on his hips, Cooper explained to Selah, "I am hoping Dream won't put the van in the same category as the trailer, but she might. I don't want to bring up any old traumas for her. Once we get her going in the training program and teach her some skills, we'll go back and redo her education on traveling in the trailer. That can't happen today."

Sweet Dream's head turned to watch Mariah climb the ramp into her roomy cargo van. Dream nickered to her new friend.

"Dream already loves Mariah. Look, she wants to go with her." Selah clapped.

Jordan came down the ramp after securing Mariah inside. As Mariah nickered back to Dream, Jordan said, "Mariah normally acts like she could care less about the other mares around, but she seems to have bonded with Dream."

Grandpa handed Dream's lead to Cooper. They walked to the ramp.

When her hoof first touched the ramp, her head shot up, and her whole body tensed.

Cooper backed her away from the ramp and worked her in a pattern designed to keep her feet and her brain busy. He tried to help her mind find a place of calmness.

When Cooper led her to the ramp again, Dream reared on her hind legs, nearly flipping over backward. The noise coming from her throat sounded unearthly. Her eyes bulged from her head, and she fought the rope, trying to jerk away in her panic. Dream's feet scrambled, throwing dirt all over Cooper.

Cooper got quiet and brushed the dirt from his jeans. "She needs time out to catch her breath."

Dream jumped and crowded into Cooper, and he popped the lead rope to back her away. "This mare is going to fight with everything she's got. That's what two years of wild on top of her trailer trauma will get ya. I don't have time today to do a trailer-loading lesson."

The horse stood trembling at the foot of the ramp.

"You have to get in, Dream. Our future rides on it." Selah rushed to her side. *Dream needs me.* "You want to try, don't you? It's okay to be scared. You have to trust me... like the sheep trust the shepherd." Selah felt the explosive tension in Dream's shoulder. "It's not going to hurt you, Dream. Trust me. I'm with you."

"Selah, I don't believe in shortcuts with horses. Another day and another time with this mare," Cooper said. "Ed, you can work her here until she trusts you enough to load. Jordan and I will be doing a clinic in College Station in three weeks. My driver, George, could come over and get her if she's ready."

What Selah heard was her summer evaporating! "If Dream doesn't go now, I will run out of vacation and have to go back to school. Oh, please try again, Mr. Cooper. I just know she can do it."

"The mare needs a lot of basic training. Then we can teach her to load without having to fight with her. You want to do what is best for her, right?"

"Yes, sir, I do. But please give her another chance."

126

Cooper exhaled. His cheeks puffed out. "I like your spirit, Selah. You are determined. That's a great quality for a young horsewoman. But your horse's not getting in the trailer today."

"I know! Mr. Cooper?" Selah pointed to Mariah in the van. "Mariah and Dream are acting like best friends. What if Mariah walks up the ramp with Dream?"

Cooper tilted his head and scratched a balding spot. "Hum... Might be worth a try. Good thought, young lady." Cooper called to Jordan. "Bring Mariah back down the ramp, turn her around to reload, and wait right there."

In a minute, all were in position. Jordan led Mariah up the ramp a step. Cooper asked Dream to follow one step. Selah, on the off side of Dream, rubbed the mare's shoulder. She put her heart in her hand and spoke calm, quiet words to the horse she loved. Then the whole party took a step backward. Forward two and back one, they inched up the ramp with Dream's nose right by Mariah's flank. Mariah gave a quiet nicker. Mariah's ear on the same side of Dream pivoted around, talking telepathically to Dream.

"The mystery to me is that so many people think horses are stupid. Stupid's not what I see here," Dad said.

"Stupid they're not," responded Grandpa. "They live by instinct, so they're highly reactive. The real problem's always people not understanding how the horse thinks."

Selah held her breath until Dream took her last step up the ramp with Mariah. Once in the luxury van, Dream quieted, and Selah exhaled a forceful puff. The mare was already reaching toward the hay that Miss Jordan had dropped into the net.

Jordan said to Selah, "I was astounded to see Mariah encourage Dream like that."

"What do you mean?" asked Selah.

"Mariah nickered and flicked her ears around to Dream. That isn't typical for Mariah. She's intolerant of any horse that close to her. Mariah would never be voted most popular in the herd."

Jordan and George set to work securing all the latches and bolts on the van. Selah stepped down the ramp with Cooper. "Her issues are fear based," Cooper said. "She's smart and has a heart to please. That combination will make her fun to work with, and I'm eager to get started. That trailer trauma will never completely heal in her. She'll load in the trailer a hundred times, and then something will spark a memory that brings the terror back. You'll have to remind her she can trust you as her leader."

"Thank you so much, Mr. Cooper. I can't wait to get to the ranch. I want to learn to be that kind of a leader for her."

As George began to close the back door to the van, Selah saw Sweet Dream with her head in the air. She was peering over the partition, looking out at Selah. "I'm not sending you away, Dream. Miss Jordan will watch over you until I can get where you are." The door to the van clunked shut, and the mare's whinny echoed in the metal transport. Selah watched the van go down the driveway for as long as she could see dust rising from the road.

The rest of the family collapsed on the deck furniture. Even the boys seemed to have run out of steam. Skunk stretched out, sound asleep.

Mom brought out tea and juice.

"Cheers to a victory," Dad declared. "I sure didn't think that horse was getting in."

Grandpa didn't let the dust settle too long. "We need to keep moving." He raised his glass of tea to Daniel. "Will you and Christopher go to the clinic to get Pearl?"

"Sure."

"Oh, lucky me, I get to hold her in the car." Christopher closed his eyes and dropped his head against the back of the chair.

Selah went to him and wrapped her arms around his neck. "You'd do it for me wouldn't you, Uncle Christopher."

Grandpa laughed.

Christopher shook his head and laughed too. "I'd hang the moon for you, Selah."

Mom packed the last covered dish in the cooler. Selah smoothed out Skunk's bed in her family's SUV and tossed a favorite toy into it. Skunk hopped up and sat in her bed. "Almost time to go, Skunk." Selah leaned into the van, cupped the dog's face in her hands, and dodged the darting wet tongue. "You keep the boys in line and don't let them drive you crazy. I wish you could come to the training center with us."

Skunk spoke to Selah. "Aarall," rumbled deep in her throat.

"I'll miss you more," whispered Selah. "If only Dream could be half as sweet as you."

CHAPTER TWENTY

*I*t seemed to Selah that the truck needed a tune-up, or
something, as slow as it was going. She tried to relax and
watch for horses in the fields, but she was too aggravated. They
could have been there an hour ago if Grandpa hadn't made so
many stops. "Not again, Grandpa. Why are we stopping this time?"

"Oh, thought I'd get a drink. Would you like one?"

"No. I'd like to get there." She put her face in her hands and
waggled her head.

"Stop acting like a twelve-year-old, Selah." He walked stiffly
toward the store.

After what seemed like forever, she craned her neck to look
into the store, wondering if he had fallen down in there and
people were stepping over him. "Come. On. Grandpa."

When he came out, he wandered over to a newspaper stand.
He bent at the waist, looking in the glass display, and appeared
to be reading the headlines.

She puckered her lips and strummed them with her finger making tiresome noises.

He dug in his pockets and dropped change into the machine.

"I'm getting old here, Grandpa. Hurry up. Hurry up." When he loaded back in the truck, she used all her restraint trying not to say what rolled around in her head. After they pulled onto the highway, it seemed the truck went even slower than before—as if that were possible.

Finally, she couldn't stop herself from saying, ever so sweetly, "Grandpa, have you noticed everyone on the road's passing you?"

"Well, they are going to pay for it at the gas pump."

Selah threw her head back to hit the headrest. "I give up."

After an eternity, they skirted around Dallas and cut through Fort Worth. Selah said, "I feel like everyone in the city is flashing by us and thinking, 'Look at those farmbillies'."

He raised his eyebrows. "If the pink princess is not happy with her mode of transportation, she may get out and walk."

Finally, the massive gate to Cooper's training center loomed before them. The blacktop road beyond the gate stretched to what looked like nowhere. Soon enough, though, she spotted a huge field full of berms, log jumps, ditches, and other horse obstacles. Several equestrian pairs trained over them.

"There are horses everywhere." Approaching the barns, Selah saw horses in paddocks, round pens, and tied to poles. Some horses walked around the poles. Others seemed resigned to their situation or had already learned to stand there and sleep.

Eyes wide, Selah pointed. "There must be a hundred yearlings." They milled around in little bands. Some grazed, some postured for first choice at the water trough, and some slept.

Another pasture held a band of broodmares, with foals of every color frolicking at their sides. "This place must be heaven." Selah tried to look everywhere at once.

Grandpa drove to the covered arena and parked. "This time of day, Cooper will be in the arena."

His guess didn't disappoint. The arena, open on three sides, allowed even a gentle breeze to keep it cool. Cooper worked one of his reining horses for several minutes before he spotted them.

Cooper waved and rode to the fence. "Ready to get started, are ya?"

"Yes, sir. I sure am."

Cooper punched the walkie-talkie secured to his shirt near his shoulder, and Jordan answered him. "Ed and Selah are here. Would you come help them get settled?"

Selah wandered the arena's perimeter, peering into the stalls. Grandpa and Cooper talked about the prospects of the horse he was working until Jordan arrived on an ATV.

"Ed, you can follow me in your truck to the cottage. Selah, would you like to ride along in the ATV?" Jordan asked.

Selah sprang onto the four-wheeler, and they rolled past the barns, all with green roofs. Jordan explained the name and purpose of each one.

"Where is Dream?" Selah asked.

"She's in the show horse barn with Mariah. It's the closest to the bunkhouse, where I live." Jordan pointed to the show barn as they passed. "There are two bunkhouses with private apartments. Usually, another apprentice stays here too, but right now, it's just me. You and your grandpa will stay in the Ritz Cottage. It overlooks one of the small lakes and is more isolated from the center's activity. If your grandpa can't stay with you sometimes, then you can stay with me if you want."

Selah smiled at Jordan, "Oh yes! That would be fun. Can we go see Dream now?"

"Let's drop your stuff first."

They pulled up in front of the cottage, and Jordan pointed out the bridle path trailhead. Soon, they'd stowed all the stuff in the cottage. "Are we going to find Dream now?"

"In a little while. Go ahead and put on the outfit you brought for the first section of filming," instructed Jordan. "Then Cooper said to tell you to come up to the house for lunch. Lunch doesn't last long around here, and he is planning on getting started right away with Sweet Dream."

Jordan wasn't kidding about lunch. Selah decided Mr. Cooper didn't actually eat—he only inhaled the fumes before he hurried back to work.

"Filming will happen on Day One," Jordan explained as they chose from the buffet table. "The camera crew always has the tape rolling. You'll get used to it, and soon you won't even notice them."

None of the staff lingered over lunch either. Selah picked an apple from the bowl as she chased out the door after Jordan. Walking briskly to the show barn, Selah stepped it up to keep pace with Jordan. Grandpa trailed along behind. "Your job every day will be to bathe and groom Dream to prep her for the morning filming. Robert will check your work because Mr. Cooper is very particular. After her lesson, you will rinse her again and clip her to her 'thinkin' post'."

"I can do that."

"I like her pink highlights, by the way,"

Selah smiled like she was being tickled and bobbed her head.

"The farrier comes to the farm every week, and she will be

responsible for keeping Dream's feet trimmed, shaped, and up to filming standards."

"She?"

"Yes." Jordan chuckled. "*She*. Your grandpa wants you to be the only one who feeds Dream, so you'll need to learn the barn schedule. On weekends, when you go home, the feed manager will take care of her. We're going to keep you busy here."

"It all sounds like fun to me."

"How much riding have you done?"

"I take a few lessons every summer. And I have a friend named Caroline, who lives near Grandpa. Her dad is the horse vet. She has horses, and I get to ride with her sometimes."

"Great. That will all help. In the beginning, Cooper will work Dream, and I'll give you lessons on our school horses. You and Dream will have your first on-camera interview today."

"I'm so excited and so nervous too."

"I understand. The horse you will train on is a gelding. He's been in the program for several years. Gringo was a mustang Cooper adopted and trained. In the cottage, there should be the DVD series of his training, if you are interested."

"Fun." Selah tried to take mental notes.

Walking into the show barn, she admired the beautiful faces that came to the stall doors to watch them pass. She looked for the one beautiful face most important to her.

Jordan kept walking down the alley, stopping only long enough to peer in at Mariah. "Dream's stall is here next to Mariah. She's already in the wash rack today as we're on a tighter than usual schedule."

When they first spotted the mare in the cross ties of the wash rack, it looked like she was drying after her bath. Her coat was soaking wet.

"Dream!" Selah froze in place. The mare stood with her head hung down to her knees. She blew with exertion. Something was wrong with this picture.

As Selah panicked and started to run to Dream, Jordan caught her by the shoulder. "Walk."

"What's wrong with Dream?" Selah tried to pull away from Jordan's firm grip.

"Looks like she tried to get the best of Robert, and she lost." Jordan called out for Robert, and the chief groom popped his head out of a stall down the alley.

"I'm coming," Robert answered.

"What did he do to Dream?"

"I can tell you, for sure, he didn't hurt her. We'll just have to wait till he finishes up and can talk to us."

Robert came out of the stall carrying his wound care kit. "That mare of yours, Miss Selah, is a force to be reckoned with. Dream was being led down the alley from her stall. She pinned her ears at Kitty Sue, our very own queen of mares. I don't know what Kitty said, but in a heartbeat, we had a rumble going on in here. The groom leading Dream is new at the center, and she lost control of the situation. Dream knocked the groom to the floor of the barn and stepped on her ankle. Then Dream went after Kitty."

Selah looked from Robert to Jordan to Dream in utter disbelief.

"Kitty was tied up and couldn't get away. I could hear Kitty squealing from the next barn. Dream bit her several times and kicked her three or four times before I could get to them." Robert chunked a roll of elastic wrap into a cabinet and slammed the door.

"We may have a new queen around here. Kitty looks like she's been in a war," Jordan said.

"It's lucky she didn't get her leg broken. Her bite marks will heal. She's lame in the left front, though, and we'll have to wait to see how it goes," Robert said.

"I feel terrible about Kitty. Is Dream all right?" Selah asked.

"Dream is fine. The new groom, on the other hand, will be walking with a limp for a while, and she quit."

"Ah, for crying out loud." Grandpa shook his head. "That makes me furious. Dream is a royal pain." He stomped down the alley to look at Kitty.

"After Dream's aggression, I had to send her to the round pen with an assistant," Robert said. "He told me Dream was wild out there and he had to keep Dream's feet moving until he could get some semblance of submission."

"Does Cooper know?" asked Jordan.

"Not yet."

"He's expecting Dream and Selah in the arena… about," Jordan checked the time, "now!"

"Dream didn't leave me any choice. Maybe you should go tell him," Robert suggested.

"Me? You should go tell him since you were involved."

"I think you should tell him. You're the head trainer. Not that I'm a chicken or anything. Cooper thinks everything that happens around here is my fault, even if I'm at home sleeping. He threatened to fire me twice last week." Robert lowered his voice, drawing Jordan along with him. "I have four kids at home, and I need this job."

"Whatever happens here is my fault," Jordan said. "Cooper pushes himself hard and just wants all of us to do our best. He couldn't manage without you, Robert."

Leaning against Kitty's stall door a good ways from the

conversation, Grandpa wore a puzzled look on his face.

Selah moved to Dream and eased her hand onto Dream's shoulder. "Why would you act like that, Dream? What have you done to us? Mr. Cooper might send us home."

From way down the alley, a voice blasted out of the arena. Jordan and Robert walked back from the arena as if on a mission. Robert slid open a stall door and led out a chestnut colt. While Robert flicked the dandy brush over the colt, Jordan put protective boots on his legs. She hurriedly ran a comb through the colt's mane and took off for the arena with him at a brisk trot.

Robert went to Dream's side, turned on the water, and rinsed away the evidence of her aggression. As the foamy salts ran down Dream's legs, Selah wondered if her dreams were washing away too. She murmured into Dream's ear, "You might have ruined everything for us."

Jordan returned and told Selah and Grandpa, "Mr. Cooper said he won't be starting Dream today."

"I was afraid he would send us home."

"Well, I thought he might too. He was pretty mad. Kitty is special around here. She's retired now, but Kitty is Cooper's mother's horse."

"Yikes."

"So you can explore the center. Get to know your way around. Meet Robert right here in the morning at seven thirty. I have to warn you, it won't take much for Mr. Cooper to decide Dream is too much trouble. He has a lot of horses to choose from, and he won't put up with grief in his schedule."

Selah felt her face pucker up like she could cry, but she gritted her teeth to not let it happen.

CHAPTER TWENTY-ONE

When Selah and Grandpa got to the barn in the morning, white soap lather already covered Dream. Selah sniffed. "You smell like a lavender flower."

Dream tilted her head and tipped her nose out. Her head bobbed in quick snaps.

"You've changed your tune about baths. The horse spa seems to suit you just fine. You look like you adore being scrubbed."

While Dream drip-dried, Robert showed Selah where they kept all the wash and grooming supplies. Then she helped him prepare Sweet Dream for her film debut. Selah combed and thinned out her mane. Robert worked all the remaining knots out of her tail. "I was convinced those knots would take me the rest of my life, Mr. Robert, thank you."

"I know a few tricks." He replaced a bottle, marked Robert's Secret Spray, on the rack.

Selah stepped back to admire the transformation. "Look at

you, my beauty queen. Doesn't she look incredible, Grandpa?"

"Just like her mother. She has that same eagle look, only her head is more refined than Harmony's."

Robert untied the mare and handed the lead rope to Selah. "Here you are, young lady. Here comes Miss Jordan after you." He hovered and kept a watchful eye on the mare's behavior.

Grandpa took a step closer too.

"You ready, Selah?" Jordan took Dream's lead rope and wiggled it to back the mare a safer distance away from them.

Selah beamed at Jordan.

"A smile like that will make a movie star out of you." Jordan smiled back at her. "Love the little pink horse monogram on your pocket."

"Thanks."

As they passed through the grandness of the show barn, Selah gushed, "I want to keep every moment of this—*forever*. I have to focus on something besides this knot in my stomach."

Jordan nodded knowingly and passed the lead rope back to Selah. Jordan stepped only far enough away to be out of view of the camera. She stayed close enough to protect Selah if Dream became a problem. They paused at the gate of the show arena, waiting to be summoned.

Dream locked up as if she was a great iron horse sculpture looking into the arena. "Don't be nervous, Dream. Everyone will love you," Selah said, reassuring them both as she rubbed circles on the mare's rigid muscles. She slipped the small green apple, which she had pilfered from yesterday's lunch, under Dream's nose.

Dream's shoulder relaxed as she crunched on Selah's offering. In unison, Selah and Dream took a deep breath and let it slowly slip out. The mare dropped her head and wrapped her neck around

Selah, as if searching her back pocket for another apple.

"Did you see that?" asked the media director.

"Not only did I see it, I already have the tape going so I got it," replied the cameraman. "The viewers will eat that up."

"The viewers? I'm eatin' it up." The media director smiled.

"No pressure." Selah watched the cameramen watching her.

Mr. Cooper motioned to Selah to bring the mare into the ring. He'd already explained how he was going to ask her a couple of questions in this first session. He introduced her and Sweet Dream to his audience. Then he explained the story of how Dream came to be running wild and how Selah and Skunk found and rescued her. He lowered his voice and energy when he talked about the death of Selah's grandmother and how Dream's mother was gifted to a dear family friend.

Selah knew the camera was rolling, and a bead of sweat from her forehead trickled into her eye. Even as the salt stung her eye, she kept a smile pasted on her face.

"So this horse was lost for two years after a trailer accident. Is that right?"

"Yes, sir, she was." The knot in Selah's stomach twisted. *Oh, please don't let me be sick right here on camera in front of Mr. Cooper.*

"When the owner was located, what did they tell you about her training?"

"She'd been halter broke and trailer loaded." Bile rose up in her throat.

"Had she had her feet trimmed?"

"Yes, and they had taught her to stand—tied—for a bath." Selah tried to keep her lunch from exploding all over Mr. Cooper.

"Had they started her under saddle?"

Selah turned away abruptly and bent over as her stomach

heaved its contents into the arena dirt. Wave after wave squeezed every—last—bite from the pit of her core.

"Oh, good grief. First, that mare beats up Kitty, and now, this. Take a short break," Cooper said. "Jordan, come help Selah." His arms pumped, and the dirt flew as he scuffed off toward the office.

Jordan was already coming down through the bleachers, two steps at a time, from where she'd been sitting with Grandpa. Jordan ushered Selah away. In the dressing room, Jordan put a wet cloth over Selah's forehead. "Lie down here for a minute."

"Is Mr. Cooper mad at me? I'm doing my best. Do you think he'll decide I can't do this?"

"I'm going to tell you a secret. I threw up the first time I was on camera too. It happens. You'll be a pro before you know it."

After a few minutes, Selah sat up. "I feel much better, Miss Jordan."

"Then let's go show Mr. Cooper what you're made of." Jordan gave Selah a big hug, and they walked out to meet the challenge.

Selah pulled her shoulders back, tilted her chin up, and tried to walk with the same power stride as Jordan. As they returned to the arena, Selah saw Grandpa walking in from the arena office with Mr. Cooper. Grandpa's stern face had a touch of red. He spun on his heel and climbed into the bleachers.

"Wonder what that's about?" asked Selah.

Jordan stayed quiet.

"Are you feeling better?" Cooper asked with a much nicer tone.

"Yes, sir. I'm sorry."

"It happens. Since we need to stay on schedule, no more food for you before taping." He smiled like a robot. "Let's try again." He signaled the cameraman.

"Before this horse was lost, she had been halter broke, trimmed, trained to be bathed and loaded into a trailer. Is that right?"

"Yes, sir."

"I would guess because of her trailer accident, she is not trailer trained anymore, is she?"

"No, sir. She's terrified of the trailer." Renewed confidence strengthened Selah's knees.

"Since you've had her at your grandpa's farm, what have you learned about her?"

"She does dressage movements in the pasture. She comes when I call her. And she kills snakes."

Cooper laughed for the camera. "Now that is talent. All right then, let's get started."

As Selah was about to hand the lead to Cooper, her stomach again betrayed her. Just dry heaves this time, but they rattled her new confidence.

"Cut!" yelled Cooper as if the cameraman didn't know what to do. Cooper motioned for Selah to leave the arena, but he didn't say a word.

She climbed the bleachers and sat with her grandpa.

He put his arm around her and whispered, "You did fine."

Selah rolled her eyes. Below them, Cooper worked with Sweet Dream, and her respect for his abilities grew. *This* was why they were here. She would just have to toughen up. Cooper was gentle with Dream. At the same time, he didn't let her get away with not doing her best. "Look how smart Dream is, Grandpa. She's learning her lessons fast."

"She does have the master teacher. He will transform Dream from a wild thing to an eager-to-please partner faster than any trainer I know."

"It's going to take a lot of hard work for me to keep up with

Dream. I can't let her down. I want us to be the best we can be together."

As if he hadn't heard a word she said, Grandpa rubbed the stubble on his jaw and muttered, "Cooper's a lot better with horses than he is with people."

Selah's eyes darted toward Grandpa, but they were the only muscle in her body that moved.

The next day, Selah watched Dream's lesson. "I'm not nervous at all today, Grandpa. I think my stomach is over it."

"Really? Easy for you to say when you're sitting in the bleachers."

"I ate breakfast. I'm going to skip lunch because my taping session with Gringo is right after lunch. Mr. Cooper told me I won't be in any more of the sessions with Dream for a couple weeks."

"Hum... We'll see how it goes then."

After Dream's session, Selah rinsed her off and tied her to the "thinkin' post". Dream processed her lesson while Selah took one of her own.

Gringo was everything Jordan had told Selah and more. "I can hardly believe that as a three-year-old he was running wild in Nevada. He looks like a dappled deer, but with black legs. What is his color called?"

"He's buckskin. He turns everyone's head when we take him to clinics. His manners are impeccable, and he always says yes to what we ask of him. He's a tribute to Cooper's training system."

Jordan rubbed the gelding in the hollow of his neck—his favorite place, judging from his reaction. "Gringo is a great teacher. He is patient with our mistakes. What I love about him is how he challenges anything 'scary'. I'd swear I've heard him say out loud, 'bring it on!'"

"Such a brave boy." Selah was trying her best to keep her mind diverted from the camera and to ignore the feeling welling up in her stomach. She swung into Gringo's saddle. The moment Jordan signaled to the cameramen to start, Selah knew it wasn't going to end well. "I'm sorry, Miss Jordan, but..." Selah leaned to the side and puked down Gringo's shoulder.

After Jordan helped Selah down and pointed her to the nearby restroom, Jordan summoned Robert, who dashed to take Gringo for a quick sponge bath. When Jordan came to find her, Selah was melting. "I can't do this, Miss Jordan. I get so nervous."

"You were so determined. But now, you're gonna quit on Dream? Don't you think Dream deserves better than that?"

CHAPTER TWENTY-TWO

As the days turned into weeks, Selah was determined to focus on the lesson and not the camera crew. Between Dream's training schedule and Selah's, there was little air left in the day. Fridays came much too fast. When she and Grandpa made the trip home, she had no idea how many times Grandpa stopped because she slept the whole way.

The next week, Grandpa couldn't stay with Selah, so he dropped her off at Cooper's with plans to return on Friday to serve as her transportation home. Since she arrived at the center, she had followed Jordan everywhere, so she was excited about getting to stay with her.

Mr. Cooper and crew were late getting back from a clinic

in Oklahoma City. Selah hung out on the porch of Jordan's bunkhouse, waiting. Feet up on the railing, she devoured one of the training manuals Jordan had assigned her. Dream's lead rope, with Dream sleeping on the end of it, draped across Selah's lap. "You've had a brain transplant, Dream. Instead of wild, you are perfect." Near feeding time, she woke Dream up. As they drifted toward her stall, the van pulled into the yard. Mr. Cooper waved and went straight to the house. Jordan unloaded Mariah, and they all walked to the barn together.

Dream moved to the stall wall between them, but Mariah turned her tail to Dream. She stood on the far side of the stall with her head stuck in the corner, cocked her hind leg, and went promptly to sleep.

"Well." Selah huffed. "She's not speaking to us, is she, Dream?"

"Don't take it personal. Mariah's been a little out of sorts. We can't find anything wrong with her. Cooper thinks she needs some time off. There's not a clinic scheduled for two weeks, so she'll get a good break. We still have time for your lesson tonight, if you'd like."

"For real, Miss Jordan? That would be great. It feels like the weekend is too long. I can't wait to get back to the center and back to work."

"I understand. All I've ever wanted in life is to spend it with horses. Coming to work for Cooper has been huge for me." Jordan hung Mariah's halter on the door hook. "It's like I feel the joy of the Lord while I'm just doing my job."

"Sweet."

"Run, get Gringo saddled, and I'll meet you in the round pen."

When Jordan got to the pen, Selah was warming up Gringo on the long line. She put him through the exercises Jordan had so patiently taught her over the last few weeks. Jordan stayed quiet and watched her little prodigy. Then she said, "Selah, you have a lot of horse sense. I enjoy working with you."

Embarrassed, Selah shifted her focus to the little buckskin gelding in the round pen. Gringo watched Selah. Both his ears tipped forward, listening intently to her melodic voice.

"Gringo has always been quite agreeable, but I've never seen him turn inside out to please someone like he does for you. Go ahead and mount up now."

Cooper slid into the top bleacher. Selah and Jordan laughed together while they worked. When Cooper came down to the arena floor, he said, "Selah, great job. Your grandma would be proud of you. You have good feel and timing like she did. She had a thing for pink too." He rubbed Gringo's neck. "And I think Gringo might be taken with you. But he's done his job, and it's time for you to work with Dream. You have a lot of talent for this. It's a shame you get sick on camera."

Selah ignored the dig and smiled with pure delight at his compliments. She'd worked hard and so had Dream. Now they would work together. "Thank you, Mr. Cooper. I've learned so much from Jordan and Gringo."

"Very good. It's time for you to graduate from kindergarten, if you promise me you will not puke all over my boots."

She fidgeted with the reins, but sat taller in the saddle. "I've not been sick since the first week."

"We start in the morning, then." He left the building.

Selah chatted nervously while she and Jordan finished up with Gringo. On the way back to the bunkhouse, they stopped by the show barn to check on Dream and Mariah.

"I have a surprise for you—soon," Selah told Dream as the

mare daintily searched Selah's pockets for a carrot. "No, it's not a carrot this time."

Jordan watched Mariah. "I can't put my finger on what is bothering her. Mariah ate all her grain, but she is decidedly annoyed and out of sorts. Something just feels wrong."

CHAPTER TWENTY-THREE

*D*ream reared and pounded both front feet on the wooden bunkhouse porch.

Selah stirred. Jordan turned on her bed and pulled an extra pillow up over her head as hooves pounded the porch again.

The sound echoed through the center like thunderous gunshots. Her whinny rang out in the night, so compelling everyone in the complex rose to the challenge.

Selah sat bolt upright in her bed. "Dream!" Terror in her heart, she tugged on her barn boots, flew to the front bunkhouse door, and ripped it open. Lights came on in the big house as she hurried to Dream. "Dream is loose! She might run away!"

"Selah, wait!" shouted Jordan, instantly awake. "Be careful! I'm coming! Wait for me!" Jordan, yanking up her jeans, sprinted right behind Selah.

The mare's hooves sprayed a cloud of dirt as she wheeled away from Selah. She thundered about thirty feet toward the barn before she reared and pawed the air with her hooves. Her piercing whinny held an urgency that drew them toward the barn like it was on fire.

"She is acting crazy," Jordan said.

Dream bolted to the barn, with Selah and Jordan running as fast as they could behind her. The mare paused at the entrance. She spun toward Selah, elevated her front shoulders, and lifted repeatedly off the ground. She popped her head up and down rapidly, as if she was beating a drum on her chest.

Everything in the barn alleyway had been dumped over, throwing halters and lead ropes across the floor. One whole cabinet of grooming supplies had toppled over, spewing shampoo across the alleyway. Bottles of different colors of goo oozed into puddles on the concrete. In several spots, they could see the imprint of two hind feet stamped onto the wood stall doors.

"What a mess. She's a destructo bomb." Jordan planted her hands on her hips as she turned to survey the disaster Dream left in her wake. "What in the world has happened here?"

"Something is wrong. Dream wouldn't just do this for nothing, Miss Jordan," defended Selah, in spite of the multicolored hoofprints stamped on the floor and the crushed bottles bearing a hoof imprint.

All the other horses in the barn were highly agitated. They paced restlessly in their stalls. The percussion of hooves making contact with the stall barriers punctuated with intermittent squeals. A whinny trumpeted through the barn, and horses all over the complex answered.

Dream now stood in her box stall next to Mariah's partition with her stall door standing wide open.

"You failed to mention that Dream is related to Houdini." Jordan exhaled heavily.

"Where is Mariah?" Selah asked as an out-of-breath Cooper ran into the barn.

Jordan sprang to Mariah's stall. "Oh, please, God, I hope we are not too late!"

With his long stride, Cooper easily covered the ground to arrive at Mariah's stall at the same time as Jordan and Selah. "What's the matter?" he asked, sucking in air. "Mariah!" He jerked the door to the stall open and dropped to his knees beside the horse.

The mare lay stretched out on her side. Her flanks heaved. Mariah snapped her head around toward her belly before it crashed to the floor again. From her throat came a low, deep groan.

Cooper rolled her lips back to look at her gums. "White," he reported. "Jordan, get on the phone to the vet immediately." He put his ear to her belly and frowned. "I'm not hearing gut sounds." He shook his head.

Selah stood frozen. From the way everyone was acting, Mariah must be in serious trouble. "Selah, grab her halter," ordered Cooper, snapping her out of her daze.

Cooper slipped Mariah's halter over her nose. He lifted her head and balanced it on his knee to ease the halter on her head. The mare sweated profusely and lay there too exhausted to hold up her head. Cooper tugged on her halter to get her on her feet, but the horse sank heavily back into the shavings.

George rushed with a huff into the barn. His shirt was open and flapping as he ran. His jeans bunched up at his ankles where he'd pulled on his boots. He pushed back his wild gray hair and repositioned his cap.

"George, move to the other side and help me get her up,"

directed Cooper. Handing Selah the lead rope, he told her, "Stay back as far as you can but keep pressure on her head." Both men heaved, and Selah hauled with all her might.

Just when it looked like they were not going to get her up, the mare summoned what little strength she had. Tucking her hind legs underneath her, she sat up like a dog.

"Don't let her sink back. Don't let her sink back," ordered Cooper.

Jordan joined Selah at the end of the lead line, and they all gave it another big effort. Dream nickered, in a soft low tone, as if to encourage her friend.

Mariah rose painfully to her feet. The stall shavings were matted to the sweaty mare. She groaned and tried to drop back to the floor.

Cooper instantly flipped the rope to startle her and change her mind. "How soon before the vet gets here, Jordan?"

"Less than ten minutes. He's just leaving a call on the Meyer Farm."

"Jordan, make Mariah walk to keep her up on her feet. Selah, stay back because she could hurt you if she goes down again. George, open the van and have it ready to go in case the vet wants Mariah at the clinic."

Cooper strode to the barn office and hit the lights for the alleyway. His worried frown hardened into a scowl as he looked around his usually immaculate barn. He walked along behind Mariah. "Keep her head up." Cooper brushed into Selah, knocking her off balance as he came alongside his mare. "Stay back, Selah. You're too close. Get down there and move that mess out of the way."

When the diesel engine noise grumbled outside, Cooper took

the lead rope from Jordan. "Run! Help the doc," he told her. "He won't have help with him at this hour of the night."

Without any formal greetings, the vet came to the distressed mare. He checked her gums and listened to her gut with his stethoscope. "Have you given her anything?" he asked.

"Nope. Waited on you."

"Okay." The vet injected the mare with a drug to relax her and another to help her with the pain. He took the pail Jordan filled with warm water. Then he lubricated the large plastic tubing, fed it up Mariah's nose into her esophagus, and passed it into her stomach. He listened carefully to ensure it didn't inadvertently go into her lungs. Then he began pumping the solution of oil and water into Mariah. She struggled against the unpleasant process, but was too weak to put up much of a fight.

Selah slipped into Dream's stall and stood at her head, waiting and watching. Selah absentmindedly rubbed little circles on Dream's neck. "Please, God, don't let Mariah die. I feel bad that I'm grateful it's not Dream fighting for her life."

Finished with what he could do for now, the vet stepped back and looked at the chaos in the barn. "You sure leave your barn in a mess, Cooper," Doc said as he gathered his stuff.

"I do seem to have a problem here," Cooper said.

George hauled Doc's equipment out to his truck. "Thanks, George. Got any coffee, Cooper? I'm going to wait around to see if Mariah's bowels will move. If not, and her pain doesn't ease up soon, then we may be looking at a twisted gut."

"Yeah, I could use some coffee too, Doc. Let's head up to the house. Jordan, when George comes back have him keep walking Mariah. I want you and Selah at the house. I'm sure Doc will be as interested as I am to hear what tornado went through my barn tonight."

Selah and Jordan eyed each other guiltily. They walked together, silently, up and down the barn alley leading a groggy Mariah. When they turned her over to George, they trudged to the house like they had all night to get there.

"He's really mad. When he's this mad, he doesn't think straight. He will blame all this on me," Jordan said. "I think I just lost my job."

"That's not fair. He won't blame it on you, Jordan. I was the one who put Dream in her stall. Mr. Cooper will send us home after this."

"No. What happens at the center is my responsibility. But I need this job. Horses are all I know."

"I'm sorry if Dream got you in trouble, Miss Jordan."

"Even if she gets me in trouble, she saved Mariah's life."

Doc sat at the wooden kitchen table with his mug of black coffee.

"Sit." Cooper pointed Jordan and Selah to chairs. "So, who's going tell me what happened here tonight?"

Jordan took the lead. "What happened is my responsibility. All I can say is I'm sorry. It will never happen again."

"That's all well and good, Jordan, but what did go down here? Just what happened in my barn?"

"Well." Jordan clasped her hands in her lap under the table. "Dream somehow got out of her stall. I guess I didn't try her latch when Selah and I left to work Gringo. Robert must not have noticed either when he did the last barn check before he went home."

"I must not have latched it," Selah squeaked. "I'm usually so careful about that. I'm just not sure. It's not Miss Jordan's fault. I put Dream away."

"Okay." Cooper held up his hand to stop their outpouring of excuses. "So Dream got out of her stall after the late barn check, right?"

"Yes, sir," said Jordan.

"I have never seen a horse be so destructive. She turned my million-dollar barn into a paintball playground? Those stains in the concrete are never going to come out!"

"Dream has never done anything like that before, Mr. Cooper. Honest. I think she was trying to help Mariah."

"By trashing the barn? Nonsense." Cooper's coffee cup sounded like it cracked when he clunked it on the table.

"I think she was trying to attract someone's attention," Jordan said.

Cooper looked at her, crossed his arms, tightened up the muscles around his mouth, and let out his breath in a puff.

Selah jumped in, "I think Dream was trying to get someone to help Mariah by making a bunch of noise in the barn. That is the only thing that makes sense. When nobody came, Dream came to the bunkhouse to get me. She reared and slammed her hooves on the deck. No one could sleep through her scream."

"I'm sure she woke the neighbors two miles away." Cooper drummed one finger on the kitchen counter like a woodpecker.

"She then ran partway back to the barn. She reared again and kept whinnying to Jordan and me. We thought she was trying to tell us something, and we went running after her. Dream was standing in her stall by Mariah's partition. We found Mariah down at the same time you did."

"Are you trying to tell me that Dream knew Mariah was sick? That she broke out of her stall and tore up the barn to get help? When that failed, she came after the two of you?"

"Yes, sir." Selah lowered her eyes to the floor. "I suppose it does sound a little crazy, but Dream is no ordinary horse."

The vet put down his coffee and stood. "I'm going to the barn to check on Mariah."

"I'll be right behind ya, Doc," Cooper said. "Selah, how would Dream even know where you were?"

"I was on the bunkhouse porch today waiting for y'all to get back, and I had Dream with me."

Starting at his forehead, Cooper rubbed his hand down over his face. He squeezed his hand and scrunched up his mouth like he'd like to contain what was about to fly out. It didn't work. "That is about the stupidest thing I ever heard. Selah, that mare of yours gives me grief every day. And tearing up my barn is the last straw." Cooper pushed his hands into his pockets and shook his head. "I wanted to do something nice for your grandpa, but I'm done."

Shocked at being yelled at, Selah couldn't even cry.

When Jordan stood to take Selah's hand, he spun to her. "Jordan, I will make a decision about your future here in the morning. Come see me in my office first thing." He marched to the front door, opened it wide, and gestured for them to leave. Jordan and Selah walked together to the apartment, and neither one could think of anything to say that would encourage the other.

CHAPTER TWENTY-FOUR

Selah, what's wrong?"

"How did you know something was wrong, Mom?"

"My first clue is that you are calling me at five thirty in the morning."

"Oh... sorry. Dream woke the whole center in the middle of the night. Mr. Cooper is so mad at her. She got out of her stall and made a giant mess in the barn. He blames it on Jordan, and he was yelling at her last night. He yelled at me too, Mom." Selah's shoulders slumped. "He said that he was tired of how much trouble we are and Dream tearing up the barn was his last straw. He was already mad at me because I get sick when we do the filming. But last night, he was scary."

"I'll come and get you as soon as I can find someone to stay with your brothers. Michael shared his stomach virus with Davy, so I can't put him in a car."

"Oh no. I'll be okay." She sank onto her bunk. "I just want to talk to you. Maybe Mr. Cooper will have gotten over being so mad this morning." *But I doubt it.*

"Selah, I don't like the sounds of any of this. This is exactly what I was afraid would happen. We never should've let you go there. We are coming after you."

"I'm sorry, Mom. Dream and I can't leave yet. Mr. Cooper has got to change his mind." Selah picked a lint ball off the army-green blanket.

"I'll talk to your dad and call you back later. You are precious to us. Nobody has the right to treat you as anything less than what you are in the sight of God."

"Thanks, Mom. I'll be okay, and it'll all blow over anyway. I gotta go."

Selah looked around the basic room, she had shared this week with Jordan. "This is a crummy room. Mr. Cooper doesn't get what she gives up to give him everything."

The center's morning rhythm was all out of whack. Selah wandered through the barns. Workers shuffled in the barns, feeding and cleaning, but there were no horses working in the training pens or arenas. It felt like someone forgot to set the alarm to wake up.

The vet's white truck drove up, and he greeted Selah cheerfully. "Good morning. How are you?"

"Good," she answered automatically and without conviction.

"How's my patient this morning?"

"Mariah looks great, like nothing happened, thanks to you."

"Thanks to Dream I got here in time, or it would be a different story and a sad day here at the center."

"It's a sad day anyway."

"What? Why?"

"Mr. Cooper is furious at Jordan, and he is sending me and Dream home."

"Oomph, I'll see about that after I check on Mariah. I should have talked to him about it last night."

Selah listened to the vet as she watched Jordan leave the center office and go to her apartment. "That's strange. Jordan should be riding her string of colts this morning." Selah ran to the apartment. She found Jordan weeping quietly as she flipped things from the drawers and pitched them into a cardboard box.

"Jordan?" She moved to her side and put her hand on Jordan's arm.

Jordan pulled her arm away. "I can't talk about it right now. I'd like to be by myself, please."

"This is so unfair, Miss Jordan." Selah turned and marched to Cooper's office. She opened the door to the forbidding building. The hallway was dark, cold, and damp. And empty. She shivered. "Lord, I need you here with me." She moved tentatively down the hallway and stopped to peer into each small office along the way. A quiet rustling of paper came from the end office where a faint light slid under the closed door.

Her hand reached for the knob, but she drew it back. *He can't do this to Jordan. I have to convince him.* She knocked on the wooden door, and it sounded like she pounded on it.

Cooper barked, "Come in."

He's still in a foul mood. She reached for the knob and hesitated again. The knob looked huge, and her hand looked tiny. *I could pretend I am a shepherd girl going up against Goliath. Except I don't have a slingshot or rocks. Besides, I don't want to kill him, just change his mind.*

The door eased open.

I don't want to go into his lair. She stepped into the dark room, lit only by a small, green-shaded lamp over his work. Cooper's back was to the door.

"What is it?" he asked without even turning. He leaned intently over the papers in front of him and shuffled them again. A distinct chill gripped the room.

She folded her jacket across her chest. "Mr. Cooper," Selah began, "I need to talk to you."

He spun around in his leather chair, holding papers in both hands. "I'm busy, Selah, and I don't want to talk to you about any of this. I'll call your grandfather soon and discuss it with him."

"Mr. Cooper, I've come because I have something to say."

He turned his back to her and refocused his attention on the papers.

Selah's face heated, and her hands shook. She would talk to the back of his head if that was how he wanted it. She launched in. "Mr. Cooper, it's not fair to take it out on Miss Jordan for something Dream did. She works harder than anyone else here. She's the first to get up in the morning to do the 'first light' barn check. She goes over your schedule to make sure everything will run smooth for you." Cooper looked up, and though he didn't turn to look at her, Selah could tell he was listening. "She helps and encourages everyone at the center. Do you know that if one of the staff is grumbling about you she puts a stop to it? She won't let anyone who works here say a bad word about you."

Cooper rotated to see her. His face was a mask.

"This whole center would shut down without her. She organizes everything and everyone. Nobody in the whole complex works longer and harder than Jordan does."

Selah struggled with what to say next. "I know I said this already, but Jordan starts work even before you do and is always the last to go to her apartment."

His face looked like a stone.

"She is your biggest fan and your biggest supporter. She's always telling us about how your techniques have changed everything in horse training. You and Jordan share the same dream. How can you cut the heart out of her? You can't send her away for something Dream did."

"You done?"

"I wanted—"

"No, I think you're done."

She turned to leave.

"Sit down, Selah," he commanded. "You have a lot of nerve for a girl your age." He put his papers on the desk and leaned forward on his arms. "You love Jordan, don't you?"

Her nod was almost imperceptible. She felt her eyes grow puffy. Biting her cheek was the only thing holding back her tears.

"Thank you for letting me see Jordan through your eyes. I haven't been able to see anything past the fact that I almost lost Mariah. You know that I picked her out as a foal? She and I have a cord, a connection between us that is rare. I trust her, and she respects me. She is that once-in-a-lifetime horse for me."

Selah sat like a rock, silent and immovable.

"I will reconsider my decision on Jordan. This doesn't change my decision on discontinuing the program with Dream. She has picked up the training quickly, but every time I turn around, she's in more trouble here. I simply don't have time or patience for that much grief."

"Dream saved Mariah's life last night."

"That is just absurd."

"No, sir. It's true. Would anyone have found Mariah until morning?"

"Everything was quiet at the last barn check."

"Would Mariah have lived through the night, if the vet hadn't come when he did?"

"Only the vet can say."

"If a horse accidentally got out of its stall, wouldn't it have just gone looking for something to eat?"

"Yes. They would've tried to break into the feed room. When that didn't work, they would've wandered in the barn annoying the other horses. Dream certainly did that much."

Selah saw the next thought hit his face before it came out of his mouth.

"In the morning, we would've found the escapee grazing on the lawn." Cooper leaned back, turning the chair slightly to look out the window at his manicured lawns. "Your whole story about Dream tearing up the barn as a call for help is beyond belief. But I can't dispute the fact that she did get out, and she did wake everyone here." He tapped his fingertips together and fell quiet.

After a few minutes of nothing, Selah got up to leave.

"Selah, it is a humbling thing for me to apologize, and I'm not a humble man. I'm told I'm better with horses than I am with people." He crumpled a piece of paper and pitched it toward the trashcan. "If you can keep that horse of yours out of trouble, you can stay."

"Oh, thank you, Mr. Cooper. We won't let you down!"

Selah left the office and hiked toward the apartment. A familiar truck, pulling an unfamiliar horse trailer, blasted up the road to the center.

"It's Grandpa. What is he doing here? He wasn't to be here until tomorrow."

He drove by her without even looking in her direction. She put her hand up to wave, but the truck roared by, headed to the center office.

"Where did he get a horse trailer? No!" Selah started running. "He's come to take Dream!"

Grandpa threw open his door, climbed out, and slammed the door behind him. He marched into the office, and that door slammed shut too. Raised voices rumbled from the office clear across the yard. She couldn't understand what was being said, but Grandpa sounded furious. "Oh no! Grandpa is going to make Mr. Cooper beyond mad again."

The voices in the office got louder. Selah made it to the office and flung open the door.

Grandpa looked like a red hornet as he turned to her. "You wait outside, Selah!"

From the force of his voice, she backed out of the office and shut the door without a sound. She could hear Grandpa now. She didn't know he knew any words like that!

The vet patted her shoulder as he passed her on the porch. The yelling stopped when he entered.

Selah tiptoed to the door and peered through the crack at the men. The vet's calm voice was the only sound. "Cooper, you're like a son to me. Since your real dad's not here to tell you, I have some things to say. Get a hold of yourself. If Mariah hadn't gotten help when she did, then she wouldn't have made it to morning. You know that mare was in serious trouble when you found her. That's what I see."

Quiet.

"Nothing else matters," the vet said. "Your beautiful barn can be repaired. You owe Selah and Ed an apology. And if you fire that young lady, Jordan, you are beyond help. She's been the best thing that's happened here."

The new hush in the office was deafening. Selah's heart thudded in her chest. Still, she couldn't tear herself away from her eavesdropping spot behind the door.

"Are you two through or do you have anything to add?" Cooper asked.

Grandpa and Doc looked at each other and shifted.

"Nah, that's it," said Doc.

"Well, you're both right. But Selah beat you to the punch. She's already laid it on the line this morning. I have been an idiot."

"As one of your oldest friends, I totally agree with you," Grandpa said.

"But I don't believe for a minute that Dream knew Mariah was sick and made that mess trying to get help."

"Maybe you still have some things to learn about horses," the vet said. "Maybe we don't give horses enough credit. Swallow some pride, Cooper, and move on."

Selah scooted away from the door as the three men walked onto the porch where she waited. Her eyes bulged out of her head. Then, catching a movement out of the corner of her eye, she turned in time to see Jordan shut the door of her truck. "Jordan, wait!" Selah dashed after her.

But Jordan didn't hear her and put the truck in gear.

The truck was rolling away, and Selah ran with all her might to catch up. She cut across the grass and pounded on the side of the truck bed. Jordan twisted around in alarm and slammed on the brakes. As Jordan opened the truck door, Selah accused her, "You're just going to leave me without saying goodbye?"

Jordan came quickly to Selah and hugged her tight. "I hate goodbye. I was hoping you would just know that I love you like a little sister, and I will miss you and my life here."

"You're not going to miss me because you're not leaving and neither am I. Mr. Cooper was super upset about Mariah. He sees things differently now."

"Not when I talked to him." Jordan looked at the three men standing on the porch. "I'm finished here."

Cooper waved to her to come to the office.

"Now what? Does he want my farm T-shirt back?"

"No, no, Miss Jordan. It's not like that."

When Jordan got to the porch, Cooper opened the door for her and pointed to his corner office.

Grandpa and Doc plopped into the porch rockers. Selah paced the porch.

After a while, Jordan stepped out, beaming like a neon sign. "Mr. Cooper is giving me a working vacation. A search and rescue team in North Carolina has asked for training help, and he is sending me. I'm going to the beach!"

Everyone was smiling as Cooper joined them on the porch. He threw his arms out with his palms up, his mouth hung open with, "Everybody happy now?"

Grandpa looked at Doc. "What do you think?"

"I was thinking Jordan should get a first-class ticket."

"You're pushing it, Doc. Selah, if Doc is right, then it might be a good idea to leave Dream's stall door unlatched in case her services are ever needed again." Cooper extended his hand to Selah.

She put hers in his and smiled forgiveness.

CHAPTER TWENTY-FIVE

*J*ust looking at breakfast, Selah felt her stomach clench and flip so she decided to skip it. *Again.* The moment she dreamed of and waited for was now. Mr. Cooper was going to put her up on Dream today. But with Mr. Cooper on a short fuse, as usual, she didn't want anything to set him off today.

Selah double-checked Sweet Dream. Dream's grooming had to be perfect for the filming. She whisked a rag over the saddle one more time. It had to be perfect too. She ran her fingers through her short hair. Her boots were dusted off, and her pink western shirt was tucked in tight. She muttered, "Don't throw up. Don't throw up."

She held Sweet Dream and waited in the arena for Mr. Cooper. "Did he forget about us? Is he even coming?" Her palms felt sweaty.

Dream eased closer to Selah, dropped her head, and cocked a hind leg.

"How can you sleep when I'm having a nervous breakdown?" She rubbed tiny circles on Dream's neck under her mane. With her fingers entwined in Dream's mane, she could feel her tension drift away.

Mr. Cooper breezed into the arena. He motioned for her to meet him in front of the cameras. Cooper gave the signal to the camera crew to begin filming, and he launched into a recap of what he'd done with Dream. Then he turned to Selah and asked, "Are you ready for your first ride on Sweet Dream?"

Delight bubbled up inside of her, bursting to get out. "Oh yes, with all my heart."

Mr. Cooper put his arm around her shoulders and drew her next to him. He smiled a real smile at her and paused as if to find his voice. When he spoke, his voice sounded a little thick. He talked directly to the camera. "Most of you know I bought Mariah as a foal. I couldn't have gotten where I am today without her. She means the world to me."

Selah was afraid to breathe or move.

"There are many things we will not understand this side of heaven. How Sweet Dream got out of her stall and woke the whole center is one of them. If she hadn't, we might not have found Mariah until it was too late. In appreciation," he said, "I have decided to establish a youth scholarship to my training academy. The Sweet Dream Scholarship recipient is to be chosen every year by Selah and myself."

Selah looked down at her boots, and her eyes blurred with tears at the gesture of gratitude from Mr. Cooper. The smile in her heart brightened her face. "Thank you!" She hugged Cooper as hard as she hugged Grandpa. "Being here with Dream has changed my life."

"What do ya say we get to work?"

Selah put her heart in her hand and rested it on Dream's neck for a moment. She sprang into the saddle and could hardly believe her dream had finally come true. *I am sitting on top of the whole wide world. Walt Disney couldn't write a fairy tale as exciting as my life is right now.*

Both of Dream's ears pointed back toward Selah. The horse stood still waiting and listening for Selah to tell her what they were going to do.

"Earth to Selah—are you ready?"

"Yes, sir. I am so ready."

"Let's put your mare through her paces, shall we? Ask her to walk and put her on the rail of the arena."

Selah started to squeeze but didn't need to do anything except lean forward a little in the saddle. "It's like she can read my mind, Mr. Cooper."

He smiled and couldn't stop. "Just go ahead and ride her around, Selah. Trot her out and do a couple one-rein stops to make sure your emergency brake is working. Then trot her along the rail and do some change of directions."

Even on their first ride, Selah and Dream worked as a cohesive team. They oozed happy and relaxed. Cooper beamed like a proud parent.

Done with the exercises, Selah and Dream trotted to the center of the ring and stopped smoothly in front of Mr. Cooper. Though she had the broadest of smiles across her face, the tears flowed freely down her cheeks.

"Mr. Cooper, thank you..."

"Selah, if you don't stop, you're going to make a grown man cry."

The blurry-eyed cameramen nodded as if they couldn't agree more.

Only one more week, and they still had a lot of work to do. They trained every morning in the round pen, followed by riding in the arena. Then Dream was tied to a pole to think about her lesson before getting some pasture time. Just because Dream was out catching some grass didn't mean Selah was goofing off.

"Jordan, you have put me up on a new horse every day this week. I feel like I could ride anything now. You have taught me so much, and I have loved every minute of it. Well, almost. Not the throwing up part."

Jordan's eyes smiled. "Yeah, no. Not that."

CHAPTER TWENTY-SIX

*I*t was Selah's last day to ride at the center. She arrived at the show arena for her lesson from Jordan, but she found Mr. Cooper there with Mariah. "I was supposed to meet Jordan here."

Cooper held the rope out to Selah. "Show me what you can do, young lady."

Selah faltered, speechless. Shaking, she reached for the lead. Realizing she was just standing there looking at Mariah, she tried to focus on what to do. She looked over at Mr. Cooper for reassurance.

He smiled encouragement to her.

"I can do this." She lifted her arm and pointed. Mariah responded by leaping with great energy. Selah was awed at the responsiveness of the amazing mare. Finishing up with the groundwork exercises, she looked to Mr. Cooper with wide eyes. "I've never had so much fun. Someday, if we work hard, Dream and I can have that something special you have with Mariah."

"You and Dream both have the talent, and now, you have the skills. Plus, you have that cuteness factor going for ya."

Embarrassed now, she smiled shyly and tipped her face away. Thinking they were finished, she tried to give the lead rope back to Cooper.

"You slacker," he mocked. "You haven't even given Mariah a proper workout yet."

"Do you mean for me to... to ride her? Nobody rides Mariah but you."

"Isn't that your saddle?"

"Oh! It is. It's my saddle! I get to ride Mariah! I get to ride a legend!"

"Well, I would strongly suggest you ask her permission, but you have mine." Cooper chuckled.

With the practiced ease of one much older, Selah lightly tipped Mariah's head toward her. With her foot firmly in the stirrup and hand on the rein, she reached for the horn of the saddle. Easing into the saddle seemed the most natural thing. And there she sat, once again, on top of the world.

"Mariah is not a statue, Selah. Go ahead and ask her to walk on," he encouraged.

She tossed him a smile and relaxed in the saddle. A joy ride was not what Mr. Cooper had in mind for them. "Put her in the cloverleaf pattern at a trot. Rest her at the barrel after two trips around."

Dutifully following his direction, she concentrated to perform the movement correctly.

"Put her into a canter on the left lead and begin a figure eight using the whole arena. When you get to the center sit deep in the saddle, and I want you to think 'right'. Turn your eyes, shift your balance and your hands to the right. At the same time, pull your outside leg back just a hair and increase your leg pressure. Let's see what happens, shall we?"

To canter Mariah was pure pleasure. She might not be a statue, but she was a rocking horse. Selah wasn't sure what was going to happen when she got to the center and did what Mr. Cooper outlined for her, but she couldn't wait to get there.

Thinking, thinking, trying... But nothing happened.

"Bring her around again, Selah, and give it another go. Add a little more rein to the right this time."

In the center again, thinking, leaning... *Go to the right, Mariah.* Squeezing with her leg and laying the rein subtly across Mariah's neck, Selah was begging, *Go to the right, Mariah.*

The mare surged upward, and they transitioned to the right, just like they knew what they were doing. Well, Mariah did anyway.

Selah got excited and, for a moment, forgot she was driving a fancy car. She shifted her weight so unexpectedly that Mariah screeched to an instant halt and almost sent Selah sailing over her head. "We did a flying lead change!" she squealed.

Laughing and shaking his head, Cooper said, "Yes, yes you did. And you almost did a flying dismount. Do you think you get to do just one? Get out there and practice."

Next, Cooper had her trotting down the line of the arena. "Turn Mariah's head toward the fence, open up your left hand, and squeeze with the opposite leg."

Then the magic happened. They were prancing in a side pass down the fence. Selah squealed again. "It's like we're dancing. It feels so light and graceful. I've never been graceful." Selah was convinced there could be no greater delight. "Mariah is magic."

"She's talented, but mostly what you are riding today is a lot of hard work over many years. Hours in the saddle and patient persistence got her where she is today. You can take Dream there if you want."

"Yes, sir. I want to so much."

"Okay, one more thing, and we're done for the day. Canter around the arena. When you get to the end, turn her to come straight down the middle toward the opposite end. Ask her to go with everything she's got. When you get about three fourths of the way down the arena, pull the reins. Release as soon as you feel her think about stopping. By the way, hold onto the saddle horn. Don't get yourself hurt on this one, all right?"

When Selah and Mariah turned in at the corner of the arena, Selah hit the gas pedal.

Mariah pounded down the arena. Power surge!

Grabbing the saddle horn with everything in her, Selah sat down and back in the saddle. Her touch on the reins was almost unnecessary, as all Mariah's legs froze in place under her. *Look at me, Grandma!*

At the stop, Mariah backed up lightly about five or six steps and stood with her head lowered almost to the ground.

"Brakes! I thought she was going to trench the arena with that stop. Every horse lover who has ever seen Mariah wishes they were me right now!"

CHAPTER TWENTY-SEVEN

*M*r. Cooper sure knew how to create a buzz. There must have been one hundred people streaming into a building that looked like a barn on the outside. Inside it looked like Hollywood. He stood on one side of the doorway. Jordan and Selah stood on the other. Some people shook Selah's hand, and others pumped it up and down.

Selah was so happy she smiled at everyone and thanked them for coming.

Mr. Cooper's wife joined him at the door. Selah's dad took a day off from work, so her whole family was here. The farm farrier arrived in a dress instead of jeans and a leather apron. Little Michael looked smitten with her. He stood with his small hands pressed down into his pants pockets and his red head tilted up at her. She smiled and nodded at him as he chattered.

Dr. Steve's daughter, Caroline, rushed to Selah's side. "Wow, Selah. I can't believe all this."

"Neither can I! I feel like a movie star. Your dad needs to come meet Mr. Cooper's vet. He saved Mariah the night she coliced."

"Only because Dream made the 911 call."

"And almost got us shipped home."

Miss Nancy Glenn was taking notes for her newspaper article. Mr. Cooper's cameramen hovered on either side of the pretty reporter, and both were trying to keep her attention. George told Selah he wouldn't miss her big event, and she watched for him. He would come flying into the theater with his shirt streaming behind him like he did the night Dream woke everyone. *How would we ever have gotten Mariah up that night without his muscles?*

Deputy Bob stepped forward and congratulated Selah. "From a lost horse to all this." He gestured around the room.

Dream's groom, Robert, leaned against the wall out of the way. "Miss Selah, it was my pleasure to take care of Sweet Dream. I will miss you."

Selah couldn't speak, so she hugged Robert instead.

Davy ran to her. "Can we get popcorn now? Can we?"

"It's over there." She pointed to the refreshment area lined with bright lights and mirrors. Overhead was a spinning, mirrored ball flashing a sparkling blue light around the room. Drinks were set out with bags of buttered, yellow popcorn and big boxes of movie candy.

Davy and Anderson zigzagged like ninjas through the vendors who advertised on the DVD, as they milled around the food court. "Selah, I'd like to send out my representative to measure Sweet Dream for our premier custom saddle."

"Really? Thank you."

"My company would like to install our horse watering system

in your stalls and pastures." Another representative handed Selah a brochure.

"Thank you. That's very nice."

"Our company would like to design a feeding and supplement regime for Sweet Dream. We'd like to furnish all her dietary requirements." A third representative gave Selah some horse treat samples.

"Carrot flavor! How did you know?"

To get to the media room, the guests passed through a gallery of poster-sized pictures of horses and riders who had trained at the center. An easel, by the main door showcased a large glossy photo of Selah and Sweet Dream on their first ride. She felt self-conscious about having their picture displayed. Flanking Selah's picture was another striking photo. It took a minute for it to register with Selah that the photo was her grandmother riding Illusion when they won the freestyle futurity.

"You look just like her, sunshine. When I look at you and Dream, I realize that I haven't completely lost her. She lives in you." Grandpa hugged her to himself.

"Grandpa, thank you for everything you have done for me. None of this could've happened without you. The only thing that would make me happier is if Grandma could be here to see us."

Grandpa put his hand out to Grandma's best friend, who was standing nearby, and drew her near to them. "What do you think, Laura?"

"I'm overwhelmed. I see the hand of God all over this. All the things that came together perfectly..."

Grandpa flipped his hand over and offered Selah a black velvet covered box. "I want you to have this."

Selah lifted the box from his hand and tipped it open. "Ah!"

Tilting her head, she smiled up at him.

"It's the buckle your grandma got when she won the freestyle championship."

"The day you fell in love with her?"

Grandpa nodded, and the tears streamed down Laura's face.

Laura leaned into Selah and whispered, "Selah, your grandma in heaven is so proud of you."

Selah threw herself at Grandpa and hugged him.

Selah sucked in her breath as she entered the media room. It had a step up for each row of seats. The rope lights on the stairs made them look like a runway at night. All the seats had arm tables for the drinks. Even though everyone was talking, the room was quiet because of the insulation on the walls. A screen the size of a real movie theater ran all the way across the front of the room. Long, heavy, red drapes folded to the sides. Light streamed from an overhead room in the back.

Selah sat on the front row, holding tightly to Jordan's hand. As Selah twisted to glare at Michael kicking her seat, she noticed Grandpa had his arm around the chair of his neighbor, Miss Katie. *That's curious.*

When Mr. Cooper walked into the theater, everyone got quiet. "I want to thank y'all for coming," he said. "I could tell you how great this show turned out, but I think I'll let it speak for itself."

With that, he sat down beside Selah. The lights dimmed and darkened. The show opened with their first day at the center.

Selah and Sweet Dream stood in the gateway, to the arena and both looked a tad overwhelmed. When Dream wrapped her head and neck around Selah, the audience said, "Aww."

Before Selah's very eyes flashed the story of her life with Sweet Dream. And this was not the end; it was only the beginning of their "happily ever after".

GLOSSARY

Bluing shampoo: whitening for white or light-colored horses

Cross tie: to secure the horse's head with a rope on each side of its halter attached to a solid wall or post with the intent to restrict movement for grooming

Dressage movements: Canter Pirouette, Passage, Volte, Piaffe

Dressage: highly controlled and precise movements of the horse and rider

Musical Freestyle: a dressage performance choreographed to music

Rocky Mountain Horse: a horse which travels in a smooth ambling gait that glides forward

Sidepass: to move the horse laterally

Tack room: storage for equipment used with horses

Teeth float: a dental procedure to smooth sharp points

Twisted gut: a life threatening, painful, intestinal condition where the colon twists—can wrap around a kidney and cut off blood flow to the colon

Warmblood: a group of middleweight horse types, primarily originating in Europe, developed to excel in dressage, show jumping, eventing

Withers: area at the base of the mane

Award Winning
DREAM HORSE ADVENTURES
Series

MARY'S SONG–BOOK 1

A girl and a foal share one thing. They are both
lame. One cannot survive without the other.

SELAH'S SWEET DREAM–BOOK 2

A girl with a dream to be an equestrian
superstar. A horse with ATTITUDE.

SELAH'S PAINTED DREAM–BOOK 3

One word can ruin a perfect life—moving.

SELAH'S STOLEN DREAM–BOOK 4

One girl's victory is the other's tragic defeat.

READER REVIEWS:

Best horse books ever. Charming. Action packed.
Heart-warming. Page turner. I'm utterly smitten.
Stole my heart. Good for the soul.

Dear Reader

Please, please share a review of this book.
Check my website for any ongoing contests or giveaways.
Sign up to be notified of the release of the next
horse adventure.

www.susancount.com
E-mail a comment: susancountauthor@yahoo.com

Follow Susan Count on Facebook:
www.facebook.com/susancount

Follow Susan Count on Pinterest:
www.pinterest.com/susancount

ABOUT WRITING...

One day...I began to write with no preconceived ideas about anything. I'd read what I had written the day before and add another scene to the adventure. No one could have been more astounded than I was when it turned into a book, then two books. The whole process gave me great joy and restored my spirit after a season of loss. My motivation was my desire to bless one particular young lady with a story to show her a love relationship in a family, with the Lord and with a horse. I truly thought the story would remain in a drawer until she was old enough to read it. Surprise!

I write at an antique secretary desk, which belonged to the same grandmother who introduced me to horse books. The desk has secret compartments and occupies a glass room with a forest view. Bunnies and cardinals regularly interrupt my muse, as do my horses grazing in a clearing.

Though I am a rider and lover of horses, I make no claims of expertise in any riding discipline. I hope my research keeps me from annoying those who would know.

The only thing more fun than riding might be writing horse adventure stories.

Saddle up and ride along!